autumn 2014

Mission

We understand "community literacy" as the domain for literacy work that exists outside of mainstream educational and work institutions. It can be found in programs devoted to adult education, early childhood education, reading initiatives, lifelong learning, workplace literacy, or work with marginalized populations, but it can also be found in more informal, ad hoc projects.

For us, literacy is defined as the realm where attention is paid not just to content or to knowledge but to the symbolic means by which it is represented and used. Thus, literacy makes reference not just to letters and to text but to other multimodal and technological representations as well. We publish work that contributes to the field's emerging methodologies and research agendas.

Subscriptions

We are pleased to offer subscriptions to CLJ—two issues per year:

Institutions & libraries	$200.00
Faculty	$30.00
Graduate students & community workers	$20.00

Please send a check or money order made out to the University of Arizona Foundation to:

John Warnock, *Community Literacy Journal*
445 Modern Languages Bldg., University of Arizona, P.O. Box 210067
Tucson, AZ 85721
Info: johnw@u.arizona.edu

Cover Art

Photograph: "CONTROL+ALT+DELETE", by Filippo Minelli. Site-specific intervention, 2007, Qalandyia Checkpoint, Israel/Palestine

> Control-Alt-Delete (often abbreviated to Ctrl+Alt+Del, also known as the "three-finger salute") is a computer keyboard command on IBM PC compatible computers, invoked by pressing the Delete key while holding the Control and Alt keys: Ctrl+Alt+Delete. The function of the key combination differs depending on the context but it generally interrupts or facilitates interrupting a function. For instance, in pre-boot environment (before an operating system starts) or in DOS, Windows 3.0 and earlier version of Windows or OS/2, the key combination reboots the computer. Starting with Windows3.1, the command invokes a task manager or security related component that facilitates ending a Windows session.

Project and artist information: http://www.filippominelli.com/ctrl_alt_delete.

Editorial Advisory Board

Jonathan Alexander	University of California, Irvine
Nancy Guerra Barron	Northern Arizona University
David Barton	Lancaster University, UK
David Blakesley	Clemson University
Melody Bowdon	University of Central Florida
Tara Brabazon	University of Brighton, UK
Danika Brown	University of Texas–Pan American
Ernesto Cardenal	Casa de los Tres Mundos, Managua
Marilyn Cooper	Michigan Technological University
Linda Flower	Carnegie Mellon University
Diana George	Virginia Tech University
Jeff Grabill	Michigan State University
Greg Hart	Tucson Area Literacy Coalition
Shirley Brice Heath	Stanford University
Tobi Jacobi	Colorado State University
Lou Johnson	River Parishes YMCA, New Orleans
Paula Mathieu	Boston College
Regina Mokgokong	Project Literacy, Pretoria, South Africa
Ruth E. Ray	Wayne State University
Georgia Rhoades	Appalachian State University
Mike Rose	University of California, Los Angeles
Tiffany Rousculp	Salt Lake Community College
Cynthia Selfe	The Ohio State University
Tanya Shuy	National Institute for Literacy
Vanderlei de Souza	Faculdade de Tecnologia de Indaiatuba, São Paulo
John Trimbur	Worcester Polytechnic Institute
Christopher Wilkey	Northern Kentucky University

autumn 2014

COMMUNITY LITERACY *journal*

Editors	Michael R. Moore DePaul University
	John Warnock University of Arizona
Senior Assistant Editor	Amanda Gaddam DePaul University
Assistant Editors	Alexandra Nates-Perez DePaul University
Copy Editors	Dana Dunham DePaul University
	Margaret Poncin DePaul University
	Bridget Wagner DePaul University
Journal Manager	Daniel James Carroll DePaul University
Design & Production Editor	Aim Larrabee DePaul University
Book & New Media Review Editor	Jessica Shumake Georgia College and State University
Social Media Editor	Melissa Pompos University of Central Florida
Consulting Editors	Eric Plattner DePaul University
	Stephanie Vie Fort Lewis College
	Rachael Wendler Univerity of Arizona

Submissions

The peer-reviewed *Community Literacy Journal* seeks contributions for upcoming issues. We welcome submissions that address social, cultural, rhetorical, or institutional aspects of community literacy; we particularly welcome pieces authored in collaboration with community partners.

Manuscripts should be submitted according to the standards of the *MLA Handbook for Writers of Research Papers*, 7th ed. (New York: MLA).

Shorter and longer pieces are acceptable (8–25 manuscript pages) depending on authors' approaches. Case studies, reflective pieces, scholarly articles, etc., are all welcome.

To submit manuscripts, visit our site—communityliteracy.org—and register as an author. Send queries to Michael Moore: mmoore46@depaul.edu.

Advertising

The Community Literacy Journal welcomes advertising. The journal is published twice annually, in the Fall and Spring (Nov. and Mar.). Deadlines for advertising are two months prior to publication (Sept. and Jan.).

Ad Sizes and Pricing

Half page (trim size 6X4.5)	$200
Full page (trim size 6X9)	$350
Inside back cover (trim size 6X9)	$500
Inside front cover (trim size 6X9)	$600

Format

We accept .PDF, .JPG, .TIF or .EPS. All advertising images should be camera-ready and have a resolution of 300 dpi. For more information, please contact Michael Moore: mmoore46@depaul.edu.

Copyright © 2014 *Community Literacy Journal*
ISSN 1555-9734

Community Literacy Journal is a member of the Council of Editors of Learned Journals.

Printing and distribution managed by Parlor Press.

COMMUNITY LITERACY Journal

Autumn 2014

Volume 9 Issue 1

Table of Contents

Articles

Poetic Signs of Third Place: A Case Study of Student-driven
Imitation in a Shelter for Young Homeless People in Copenhagen..................1
Christina Matthiesen

Community Engagement in a Graduate-Level Community
Literacy Course...18
*Lauren Marshall Bowen, Kirsti Arko, Joel Beatty, Cindy Delaney,
Isidore Dorpenyo, Laura Moeller, Elsa Roberts, and John Velat*

Discordant Place-Based Literacies in the Hilton Head,
South Carolina Runway Extension Debate... 39
Emily Cooney

Civic Disobedience: Anti-SB 1070 Graffiti, Marginalized
Voices, and Citizenship in a Politically Privatized Public Sphere................. 62
Veronica Oliver

Book & New Media Reviews

From the Book Review Editor's Desk 77
Jessica Shumake, with editorial support from Jim Bowman
Anthony D. Boynton, II and Saul Hernandez, Interns

Keyword Essay: "Critical Service Learning" 79
William Carney

The Unheard Voices: Community Organizations and Service Learning
By Randy Stoecker, Elizabeth A. Tryon, with Amy Hilgendorf, eds..................84
Reviewed by David Dadurka

*Circulating Communities: The Tactics and Strategies of
Community Publishing*
By Paula Mathieu, Steve Parks, and Tiffany Rousculp, eds................................88
Reviewed by Beth Savoy

Zines in Third Space: Radical Cooperation and Borderlands Rhetoric
By Adela C. Licona..92
Reviewed by Jenna Vinson

The Word and the World: The Cultural Politics of Literacy in Brazil
By Lesley Bartlett...96
Reviewed by Katie Silvester and Anne-Marie Hall

Poetic Signs of Third Place: A Case Study of Student-driven Imitation in a Shelter for Young Homeless People in Copenhagen

Christina Matthiesen

During a series of writing workshops at a shelter for young homeless people in Copenhagen, I examined to what extent the literary practice of student-driven imitation with its emphasis on self-governance and a dialogical approach can engage marginalized learners in reading and writing. I found that student-driven imitation had the potential to engage different kinds of writers and that they adopted the practice with ease and confidence. In addition, I experienced that the residents' preferred genre was poetry and that they generally sought a neutral space with low attention to social status, characterized by dialogue and a homely feel. This space is comparable to Oldenburg's third place, and I suggest that poetry is a textual marker of this space.

> Reading, however, is free.
>
> —Quintilian (X.I.19)

Clearly, it began with an idea. Not an explicated need. Not an invitation or request. Actually, I ended up insisting, mostly out of curiosity, but some stubbornness might have been at play. My idea was cultivated from two interests especially: my exploration of imitation as delineated by Quintilian; and my attraction to the public turn of composition as scrutinized by Elenore Long and developed by Linda Flower and Paula Mathieu, amongst others, as well as the ethnographic work of Ralph Cintron. My exploration of imitation as delineated by Quintilian had led to the development of a concept I call student-driven imitation (Matthiesen 5). Student-driven imitation foregrounds the choice and reflection of the individual student: "Which texts fascinate me, and what do I need or want to learn?"

Here, I will tell a story of what happened at a shelter for young homeless people in Copenhagen, where I held a writing workshop series of thirteen sessions based on student-driven imitation. My aim was to examine if, and to what extent, student-driven imitation has the potential to engage marginalized learners in reading and writing. These learners may be with or without learning disabilities, but typically have negative, or poor, educational experiences due to difficult life situations, and therefore may struggle with reluctance towards learning and low confidence levels.

Imitation exercises from the classical rhetorical tradition are seldom seen in community literacy projects, maybe due to their often restricted pedagogical scope, which focuses primarily on pattern practice (see D'Angelo; Glenn, Goldthwaite, and Connors; Terrill; and Fish). However, student-driven imitation foregrounds a practice based upon the students' own choices of text and an unrestricted interaction, in which mirroring is not the goal but process is. This practice, I claim, has the potential to engage marginalized learners in reading and writing, since it is highly inclusive of the experiences and reflective practice of the individual learner, and emphasizes the decision-making of the individual learner as a reader and writer, her preferences, goals, and manner of interaction.

Where imitation exercises generally build upon the reciprocally reinforcing relation between reading and writing (Nelson 437; Salvatori 659), as well as train dual attention to both the learner and the text (Terrill 297), student-driven imitation also strongly asserts the premise of *dialogism*, as developed by Bakhtin, naturally dependent and receptive to what has already been said and written (Bakhtin 276). This is reflected in the five dimensions of student-driven imitation: "1) Paying attention to FASCINATION", "2) Identifying QUALITIES WORTH IMITATING", "3) Carrying out CRITICAL REFLECTION", "4) Considering ACCEPTANCE", and "5) Exploring ways of INTERACTION" (Matthiesen 79-83). The dimension of interaction animates unrestricted interaction across genres, and situations: a blog post may stir up a poem, and the other way around. Maybe a perspective was found useful, maybe a metaphor, maybe just a word, maybe only if twisted or mocked. In this manner, student-driven imitation, as a literate practice, seeks to strengthen rhetorical agency: that is, both rhetorical skills (as restricted imitation exercises) and the ability to find or create rhetorical opportunities (Hoff-Clausen, Isager, and Villadsen 57), by becoming attuned to and grant agency of others (Geisler 15; Flower, "Public Engagement" 202). In Michael Warner's sense of what constitutes a public, self-organized attention to and reflexive circulation of discourse (Warner 419), the literate practice of student-driven imitation can be viewed as "a mode of public engagement" (Asen 191). Thus, student-driven imitation as a literate practice not only underscores the experience and goal-setting of the individual learner, but is based upon participation in public life through reading and writing. Hereby, the practice resembles key principles in Dewey's thinking on education: impulses, experiences, and goals of the learner are central and must be linked to concrete action, inquiry, interaction, and participation in public life (Dewey, "Democracy" 101, "Experience" 33). But student-driven imitation also contains an aspect of Freirean pedagogy, which seeks a dialogue not dominated by authoritarianism, alienating intellectualism, but instead animates a dialogue in which students hold power as subjects (Freire 67). This contrasts to "banking education," in which the teacher preserves knowledge (61). In the subject of rhetoric, language itself is the core content of the education, but in contrast to other educational content, language is free and renewable for everyone. Yet, as Deborah Brandt, inspired by Bourdieu, reminds us, language is often made scarce and hard to get (769). Student-driven imitation seeks to acknowledge and foster receptiveness to both the language and invention of the individual and of the other, "elite and street, canonical and vernacular" (Matthiesen 90). One cannot do anything wrong when working with student-driven imitation, and one can work with student-driven imitation on one's own, attuned to the individual talent in everyday life – all one needs is pen and paper. Thus the literate practice seeks to promote independence, confidence, and a sense of agency, important properties for all types of writers, especially those on the margins (Alberti 391). In addition, working with the concept does not depend, at least in the long run, on teachers, technical support, or funding. Once explained and tested, the student can work with student-driven imitation on her own.

As we shall see, student-driven imitation as a literate practice has the potential to include and engage writers on different levels, and is easily adopted. What I did not foresee, though, was the residents' preferred genre, poetry. Nor that they would generally seek a dialogue with me, and the other residents, characterized by a low attention to social status, playful moods and a homely feel, in which conversations about reading, writing, education, and politics could unfold, and conflicts and anger surface. This dialogic space is comparable to the sociologist Ray Oldenburg's third place. The concept of third place is bound to urban informal public spaces, such as the barbershop, the pub, the gym, or the street, places we seek between our first and second place, home and work. It is characterized by open, neutral ground, voluntary recurrent participation in, primarily, dialogue, low attention to status, playful moods and a homely feel (Oldenburg 22–38). In line with Dewey's view on communication in local communities (Dewey, "The Public" 153), Oldenburg sees great democratic potential in third places: here a community can take shape, connect, and built up, "give substance and articulation to group sentiment" (75), but he also underscores the personal benefits of the third place: it promotes "novelty," "perspective," and "spiritual tonic" (Oldenburg 44–55). I find Oldenburg's concept relevant here, because it emphasizes, besides dialogue, open, neutral ground, recurrent voluntary participation, and low attention to status.

The emergence of a space comparable to the third place was marked, I propose, not only by the nature of our physical recurring meetings in the shelter, but by the residents' preference for poetry, a genre of neutral ground and with low attention to status, as opposed to telling one's own story or writing job applications.

I begin with an account of the setting and set-up of the workshop. Then, I exemplify how student-driven imitation can work in relation to poetry and specify the residents' strategies for interaction. This leads to an illumination of the value of poetry in relation to student-driven imitation. Next, I point to other signs of engagement, from anger to conscientiousness and curiosity, which may have been triggered by the dialogic approach of the concept and workshop. Finally, I discuss how strengths of this open-ended version of the literate practice may also be a weakness and conceivably induce a feeling of lack of progress and purpose. This leads to an outline of strategies of possible value to future projects.

The Setting and Set-up

An often-used, informal term for young homeless people in Denmark is "sofa-surfers". This term points to the fact that young homeless tend to hide their homelessness and avoid the most obvious and often rough places sought by adult homeless, such as the most well-known shelters and street corners where they sell the homeless' newspaper. Thus, these young marginalized people often live a hidden life away from institutions, treatments, and social and educational activities. According to the social workers that I have been in contact with, this group of young people typically see themselves as simply lacking a place to stay, not as homeless people with all their accompanying connotations. Nor do they look like homeless persons in the sense of the stereotypical image: a homeless man with a dog and three plastic bags, sleeping on a bench in a park. This ought not, however, lead us to conclude that the lack of a place to stay is their only problem. Many suffer from the same problems as the majority of non-immigrant homeless in Denmark. Besides economic poverty, these problems include social, personal, and interpersonal problems, such as a general distrust of others; problems with attention and concentration; alcohol and drug abuse; intense angst, and, sometimes, psychiatric issues such as psychosis and schizophrenia. A fairly new initiative to meet these vulnerable, marginalized young people is RG60, a shelter and dwelling place for young homeless between 18 and 30 years of age, established in 2010, and located in the area of outer Nørrebro in Copenhagen.

To enter RG60, you must ring the bell and wait for one of the social workers to open the massive black door. A camera is placed above the door in a small gate. From the gate, behind a fence, you get a glimpse of the yard. RG60 is both a shelter and a social service offering accommodation for up to six months, sometimes longer. All residents can use the large living room, and unlike most shelters for homeless people in Copenhagen, the living room may be used 24 hours a day. When entering RG60, you immediately step into the front part of the living room. Here, you find table tennis, table football, two or three locked-in computers, and a small room for video games. The other part of the living room contains sofas, a TV, and a long table used for meals and house meetings. The walls are covered with paintings made by the residents, from dreamy blue flowers to graffiti-like patterns. Usually, the living room is not used until around 1 p.m. or later, when the residents either return to the house after having done errands or get out of bed. The vast majority of residents have no jobs or education.

RG60 was a relevant and compatible partner for many reasons: their focus on the growing number of young homeless people in Denmark; their guidelines, which give residents the possibility of staying, not only at night, but during the day, for periods of up to six months and sometimes longer; their allocation of funds to offer young homeless a place to stay and an action plan with contact to caseworkers but no regular in-house pedagogical activities. Finally, my project matched the founding principles of RG60: participation and self-government.

My initial meetings with the staff and the director were characterized by positive responses. It turned out that RG60 fairly often receives requests from institutions that wish to work with them. Most often these invitations are turned down, since they rarely point towards actually engaging and supporting the residents. Encouraged by this opening, I visited RG60 a couple of times to hang out and get a sense of the place and talk with the residents. Few of them showed any interest: typical responses ranged from "Who are you, don't you think we can write?" to "I do not like writing at all." Despite this apparent reluctance from the residents, I decided, with the director's approval, to explore what would happen if a workshop was actually set up. This decision was in part inspired by Flower's work with urban high school students with learning disabilities: "For them, rhetoric is an embodied act that opens them to being co-opted by the discourse of disability in which they become the object of its rhetoric, not a rhetorical agent" ("Going Public" 138). Of course, I could not presuppose that all residents had learning disabilities; some had, I knew. I did not meet the residents with questions about their baggage, but instead with an invitation to write. I wanted to get a chance to show the residents that this project sought to build upon and strengthen what people actually can do instead of what they cannot do, and to work with a rhetorical approach to reading and writing, that is a holistic, functional and purposeful approach, foregrounding meaning-making instead of teaching fragmented skills (Flower, "Going Public" 140).

Our plan ended up looking like this: nine writing workshops were to be offered in February 2011 at the long table in the living room each Monday and Wednesday, from 1 p.m. to 3 p.m. At the end, and upon request, we prolonged the workshop series with four additional sessions, of which no one came to the last two. Each workshop was setup to be based upon student-driven imitation and include related kick-about exercises of various kinds, dialogue, and response. Participation in the workshop series was not binding. The residents could drop in halfway through the workshop series, or in the middle of one workshop, and attend one or all workshops. At a subsequent house meeting, I presented the workshop. It was entitled *Strong words*.

The project was designed in an action oriented research manner, that is, grounded in dialogue, concrete action, and reflective practice, allowing all participants room for intervention in order to shape content, goals, and process (Lewin 38; Huang 99; Rönnerman 19), much in line with the pedagogy of Freire. As is significant for action research, the project was aimed at exploring and developing a new experience and a possible new practice for all participants: residents, staff, and myself as a writing educator with a special interest in the concept of student-driven imitation.

The material for this investigation is my logbook and workshop plan. Having my logbook as a source for the study gives the account an autoethnographic touch. I will present glimpses of the world of RG60 and the workshop series in order to tell, not the whole story, but an integrated and balanced one.

Initial Experience: The Blend of Public/Private and a Glimpse of the Third Place

On Tuesday nights, RG60 have their house meetings. Sometimes they last ten minutes, sometimes thirty. Updates are given. Disputes discussed. Afterwards they clean the house for about fifteen minutes. On such a house meeting, two weeks before the first session of the workshop series, I presented the workshop. The staff did not indicate that residents could sit still for very long, so my presentation had to be brief and engaging. With me I had a poster for the workshop series, a visualization of the concept of student-driven imitation, and pens, and post-it pads. Inspired by Andre Breton's surreal parlor game, my plan was to get them to write just one half-sentence each. Every other person is supposed to write an if-phrase, while the other half writes a so-phrase. Afterwards, the phrases are read aloud and combined into a sentence by the person sitting next in line. I wanted to explore if they would walk away from the task, as I had been warned, or actually write, and, if so, whether they would groan or feel excited. As is the case of student-driven imitation, Andre Breton's surreal parlor game is about connecting words and writers in a free manner. The surreal parlor game especially highlights chance and attentive listening, and often evokes unexpected creation of meaning and joy.

Eleven residents participated in the house meeting: Four girls, seven boys. Some smelled of alcohol. On the table was stale cake from the local bakery. "Please, have some cake," they said. Five minutes later, the floor was mine. With the poster in my hand, I presented the workshop series. "None of us escapes language," I said, "the language of others, the language of ourselves, therefore we should approach language with a conscious attitude and train our awareness and skills as readers and writers." I stressed that the workshop would combine reading and writing attuned to their interests and needs, from job applications to poetry. They seemed to listen. I was surprised by their attention. Then, one said, "Don't you have a poem with you?" In my bag I had a short poem by the Danish poet Lars Skinnebach, desperate and philosophical.

"Read it again," they say. Some of them want to see it. We talk about it, its meaning and words. Who is egocentric? A girl, F, wants to keep it. Shortly after, I present the visualization of student-driven imitation. Their attention, I feel, is more polite. Then, I hand out post-it pads and pens. Some look skeptical. Then they write. No one leaves the table. I am thrilled to see them all putting pen to paper. Then we combine their phrases. They listen to each other. Applaud. Laugh. They seem excited to read their own phrase aloud. One boy, B, has written several sentences, full of rhythm and rhyme. He is eager to read it aloud. It is beautiful and philosophical. Everyone seems surprised.

While they cleaned the house, I put up posters for the workshop. Quite a few spoke to me, stressing that writing is important, that Danish grammar is a struggle. They would like to work with songwriting and poetry, they told me. One wanted to work with job applications.

Between the house meeting and the first workshop session, I visit RG60. The residents are talkative. Two of them are painting. One comes by with a plate full of scrambled eggs. "Do you want any?" he says before he sits down and grabs the daily newspaper. The conversation turns from the other day's documentary on Egypt to personal stories about having no contact with relatives. When I unlock my bike outside the house, three of them are smoking a joint the size of my thumb. "See you Wednesday," they say, and look as if we have an appointment.

So, did they sit and wait for me, ready with pen and paper, five minutes to one on the day of the first workshop? Of course not. I did not expect them to, either. Three residents were in the living room; one is sitting at one of the two computers in the house, the other two, V and S, are watching a film with Charles Bronson. None of them wants to participate. Their turning away is polite and firm. After a while, they leave the room for a smoke. There I am, sitting in the sofa, wondering what to do. I look at the clock on the wall. It is 13.30.

Then, through the windows I get a glimpse of F. She is in the office talking to one of the social workers. Maybe she would like to participate? I will have to wait to find out. Energized by this, I move to the kitchen, just to have a look. There is K. He wants to participate. Meanwhile, S has turned up in the kitchen. He tells me about his experiences with school: about always behaving well, but not being able to concentrate. He does not know his age. He would like to sit with us and listen. We place ourselves at the long, worn wooden table in the living room. F is there now. She does not know whether she wants to participate or not, but she will sit with us and eat her lunch, rye bread with liver paste. It is two o'clock in the afternoon now. There are a handful of residents in the living room watching television. They do not want to participate, but they are paying attention to what is happening at our table. I have the feeling that they are paying attention even with the back of their heads.

K, S and F want to know where I am from. I tell them about my project, about rhetoric, its educational tradition. K wants to improve his song writing. He already has several drafts on his computer. He agrees to bring them to the next workshop. F wants to work with poetry. She admires the beautiful sadness of Tove Ditlevsen's poetry and the snug humor of Benny Andersen's. F makes us a cup of tea. Then, she goes to her room and returns with four notebooks. Somewhere in one of them, there is a poem that she would like to show me. It is a poem she has written some years ago. It is about a burning candle. A young man appears. He wants homework. All of us agree to bring a text with us to the next workshop. K a song. F a poem. I will bring both. The guy that wanted homework has walked away. F and I are shaking hands. She is looking forward to choosing a poem, but she is not sure if she can come to the next workshop because of the Super Bowl. I will be here, I say. Hm. Are we on a roll now? And if so, how and where to?

These initial experiences show that the residents do have an interest in writing, an interest that does not seem apparent when they are asked point blank about writing, but which appears when they have writing presented to them. The house meeting as well as the first workshop session indicate that this interest in writing is fragile, easily ignited and just as easily forgotten or rejected.

Also, these initial experiences underscore the fact that a shelter is a mix of the private (a living room with remarks such as "have some cake") and the public (an institution with staff and rules), zones that the Western tradition commonly has understood as spatially distinct (Warner 26). The concept of student-driven imitation is a blend too, mixing and bridging private and public: the starting point of student-driven imitation is the fascination of the individual, but the texts are public, circulated and open to everyone. Likewise, the concept calls for personal reflection as well as interaction outside the home - see Warner's list (29). Certainly, it is not unique that private and public are intertwined: "Public and private are not always simple enough that one could code them on a map with different colors – pink for private and blue for public. The terms also describe social contexts, kinds of feelings, and genres of language" (Warner 27). Thus, they are merely hosts of norms and contexts that intersect, evolve and differ in culture and time, and are regularly challenged: in Western politics, for instance, by former counter publics such as women's and gay movements (Warner 51), in theory by such as Hauser's concept of vernacular rhetoric. Maybe we even have social contexts and genres of language where private and public not only blend, but actually merge. Such social contexts could be Oldenburg's third place. For Oldenburg, though, the third place is an open physical space: the pub, the street. But if, as Warner proposes, we instead link public and private not to space, but to social contexts, types of feelings, and genres of language, then I propose that private and public merge in the third place, and that an example of such a textual genre could be poetry, the residents' preferred genre, characterized by third-place traits such as an open neutral ground for dialogue, low attention to social status, playful moods, and a homely feel.

Poetic as in Poetry: Confidence, Dual attention, and Public Discourses

On a roll was certainly not the right expression. Particularly at the beginning of the first couple of workshop sessions, I started out with a tour around the house asking if anyone wanted to join the workshop. The number of participants fluctuated between one and five. Three participants became regulars: the girl F, and two guys, B and V. F, age 26, was a high school graduate with two years of additional education. B, age 20, had dropped out of high school more than once. V, age 22, had never entered high school. He had quite successful work experience as a telephone salesman. They represented three levels of literacy: F was a relatively skilled writer, accurate and with a talent for rhythm and suspense. V was untrained and unaccustomed to writing, but possessed basic formal writing skills. B, on the other hand, had problems with basic formal writing skills such as spelling and coherent sentence structure, but he had a copious vocabulary and was eager to communicate in general, and also in writing.

Increasingly, other residents would come by, sit down and listen, join the conversation, talk about reading and writing, education and politics, sometimes about family life and experiences at institutions. When asked directly about what kind of texts they would like to work with, the answer was poetry.

Poetry, as opposed to the telling of one's story, provides a neutral ground, with low attention to social status, where private and public merge. The writing space of poetry is both personal and universal: it is a genre that strongly stresses the individual temper and at the same time, with its implied fictional distance acquires a universal character. In this free writing space, inquiry and expression can unfold while escaping some of the demands of fiction and persuasive writing in terms of length, coherence, conventions, and grammar. Poetry per se is a right to shape your own language.

As inherent in the concept of student-driven imitation, the residents were themselves supposed to bring texts to the workshop, based on their fascination as readers and reflection as writers. This happened only once, when F brought a poem by a former fellow student at a boarding school, about a little girl in a children's home.

At the end of the third workshop, we agreed that for the next workshop I would bring ten different poems. I chose poems that differed in terms of theme and form. All of them were fairly short, one page, and written between 1920 and 2009 by Danish poets.

On the long table are ten poems. In turn, we, that is, B, F and I, pick a poem and read it aloud. We respond spontaneously to each poem. Meanwhile, V shows up. He wants to see what we are doing. "But I am not going to read it aloud," he says. The others pick a poem again and read aloud. Afterwards V, too, reads a poem aloud. They read aloud with care and concentration, shaping words in their mouth, some of which they are not familiar. They listen to each other and easily grasp and describe the emotions at stake in the poems – from Leth's poem about controlling the body, competition, and performance, to Hammann's poem about the trivial acts of a well-behaved person, foreshadowing not only frustration but an animal underneath.

After having read all ten poems aloud, they each pick a poem for student-driven imitation. We are going to work with the following dimensions of student-driven imitation: fascination, qualities worth imitating, and interaction. F sticks to the poem that celebrates love; V picks a surreal poem; and B picks the poem about the trivial acts of a well-behaved person. With a green marker they now underscore ideas, subjects, lines, and words that fascinate them. All words are shared and unfolded – from the idea of the lover as a surveyor and the word "life doubler" (F) to lines such as "do I fall out of society and into a dream" and "The stars are psychotic children" (V). Then, with a blue marker, they underscore ideas, subjects, lines, and words that they find worthy of imitation. Overlaps appear. Newfound aspects are valued. The findings are shared and unfolded. Subsequently, they start writing their own poem, inspired by the poem that they have worked with, and by their findings. I stress that they can do whatever they feel like: quote, twist, mock, choose to reuse the theme or just a word.

After a while, they read their poems aloud. V has interacted with the surreal poem in a *mimetic* way, reusing the theme and style in a loyal manner, even quoting a few lines, but adding rhyme at the beginning of the poem. F has interacted with the homage to a beloved person in an *inspirational* but independent manner, reusing the theme, skipping the surveyor metaphor, using a more straightforward style, adding rhyme throughout the poem, reusing the word "life-doubler" at the end as in the source text. B, on the other hand, has interacted with the poem about civilized behavior in an *antagonistic* manner, twisting the theme by underscoring the idea that comparing human to human is far more important than comparing humans to animals. B's poem goes even further and ends with a reflection on how the responsibility of man constantly increases.

These imitation strategies illustrate that the residents easily interacted with their poems in a free self-governed manner. They each independently found and shaped a strategy of imitation suitable for their individual temper and intention and expressed joy over their processes and results. They did not need a presentation of already listed strategies, as for instance *following, transformation, eristic*, all taken from literary imitation practice in the Renaissance (Bender 345). Immanent in the literary imitation strategies of the renaissance is the source text. This is the case too with the restricted imitation exercises in rhetorical education: memorization, translation, and paraphrase (Corbett 246; Sullivan 13; Terrill 305). The restricted imitation exercises may train both comprehension and sentence structure (rhetorical skills), but they allow little room for the individual temper, situation, and intention (rhetorical capacity). On the other hand, I argue that the fourth typical imitation exercise in rhetorical education, close analysis (Corbett 245; Sullivan 13) holds the potential to train both skills and capacity, at least if the source text is used in writing as a means of invention in relation to individual temper, situation, and intention. Here, mirroring is not an end in itself, inspiration is.

In line with Quintilian's notion of imitation and the concept of student-driven imitation, the crucial starting point is pedagogical, and the aim is inspiration. Thus, the outcome in relation to the source text can be more or less mimetic, more or less atomized, even to a degree where it is hard to trace the source text. Hence, an endless variety of imitation strategies can materialize.

As illustrated in the varied imitation strategies of the residents, the process of interaction came easily, naturally, and with unpredictable and diverse results, both in terms of invention and style. These strategies are far from pattern practice, even though pattern was studied. The strategies may overlap, as is the case for instance with the antagonistic and inspirational strategy. An outline of a typology is not within my scope here; instead, I would like to highlight fluctuation and hybrids as premises for student-driven imitation – as is the case with traditions of imitation generally (Muckelbauer 66; Warnick 128).

So, what value does poetry hold in relation to student-driven imitation, besides sharing and underscoring a need for a right to one's own language and a space that is both private and public, in which one can act independently, with confidence, and a sense of agency? I think two aspects are worth highlighting, 1) the dual attention and dialogic interaction of imitation in itself as valuable, and 2) the literary genre's potential to reflect, explore, and play with multiple public discourses, as delineated by Bakhtin (292).

Concerning the first, in all text-based imitation a dual attention of the student to both a public text and to herself and her own writing is fostered, thereby anticipating a democratic stance: "*Imitatio*, as a tenet of rhetorical pedagogy, is as central to the tradition as two-sided debate and strategic effacement, but less often noted as valuable for the crafting of democratic citizens" (Terrill 300). What Terrill highlights is the stance and movement of duality in imitation, not a specific discourse. Hence, the process of imitation in general is valuable, regardless of the choice of discourse, poetic or political, from the past or from the present. Especially, I argue, unrestricted imitation strategies, as opposed to the restricted strategies Terrill highlights, promote a dual attention with a rhetorical approach, in contrast to a technical.

Concerning the second, the literary genre's potential to reflect, explore, and play with multiple public discourses. I stress that poetry and fiction should not be set aside in relation to public discourses. Literary language can "unite in itself parodic stylizations of generic languages, various forms of stylizations and illustrations of professional and period-bound languages, the languages of particular generations, of social dialects and others" (Bakhtin 292). Only a few of the ten poems in our workshop happened to have such polyphonic traits of recurrent public discourses, but focusing to a higher degree on such poems could be worth exploring.

Poetic as in Imagination and Deep Feeling: Dialogue, Discovery, and Trust

Despite the fact that all three residents, B, F, and V, ended this session of student-driven imitation by selecting two poems each for future work with books by the poet whose poem they had interacted with, this kind of thorough work with student-driven imitation did not happen again. I naively envisioned us moving up a level towards some kind of mastery as if we had our feet on a ladder. I envisioned posters with their poems in the living room. A reception. But our feet were on slippery stones at the sea. And what I had not envisioned was anger.

At the following workshop, B and F participated. B's body was boiling. Legs pumping against the floor. He delivered a long, seemingly unstoppable monologue of frustration: over people in power, relativism in general as opposed to one religious truth, the written word as sacred, and untouchable, the workshop, the assumption that rhetoric could make a difference, democracy. I naturally wanted him to turn his words into writing. That would also force him to slow down and focus, as well as explore his ideas. B, being especially frustrated with the lack of justice in a democracy, became highly upset when I suggested he should write about it: "Do you want the Secret Service to come after me? I don't want to put anything on this subject to paper. Are you crazy?"

Generally, the workshop sessions at RG60 were unpredictable on every level. I did my best to adjust to the current situation and the residents' reactions and requests, from anger to a wish at the end for prolonging the workshop series. Repeating the moves from the fourth workshop did not appeal to them. Instead, I came up with exercises that supported the literate practice of student-driven imitation stressing self-governance and especially dialogue. Alongside this, F pursued through the workshop series her newly found interest in haiku poems, while V worked with descriptions of his hours at job activation. In both cases, I assisted with text examples and feedback. Below, I will describe three exercises that in different ways support the literate practice of student-driven imitation:

Connect to a Sentence You Come Across: 'You and Publics Around You'

Since I wanted to know more about their attention to whatever publics, and I wanted them to pay attention to words and texts around them as both readers and writers,

I asked them to find sentences that somehow appealed to them or set their mind in motion and, in a free manner, use the sentences as starting points for their own writing. Between Wednesday and Monday, they were asked to find four sentences, write each sentence at the top of a paper, including its source, and then write their own text below. B did not choose sentences, but words: power, justice, love, and his interaction led to some well-written aphorisms. I was allowed to read but not to comment on his writing. F had found sentences in mainstream online newspapers, silly headlines that annoyed her, and her interaction lead to chatty elaborations of the silliness, as if she were talking directly to the media behind. This exercise supports the principle of self-governance in student-driven imitation as well as the dimensions of both fascination and interaction.

Collaborative Story Writing: 'You and I and Our Imagination'

In the middle of one of B's outburst of anger, for some reason—out of the blue, actually—I suggested we write a story together. He accepted this invitation. He wrote one passage; I wrote the next. A story of a wounded soldier took shape. This dialogic way of writing forced both of us to read, understand, and connect with the writing done by the other. In this manner, I found a pathway to comment on his writing, whenever I had a good reason, with regard to problems with grasping the meaning, typically because of missing words or misspellings. This exercise highly supports receptiveness to the words of another, a basic premise of student-driven imitation, as well as the dimension of interaction, stressing especially coherence and surprise.

Chreia: 'You and Your Expansion of Famous Quotes'

With the ambition to engage more residents and examine their reaction to a more directive set of rules, I introduced the classic progymnasmata-exercise *chreia* (Kennedy). I brought in quotes by Disney, Woolf, and Cohen, amongst others. In this session five residents participated, selecting their favorite quote, struggling with the elements in the *chreia*, from praise and paraphrase to example and testimony, all of them expressing both frustration as well as excitement over working with a strict form. The *chreia* was compared to a puzzle, releasing a feeling of fulfillment when every bit ended up fitting together. As in the case of student-driven imitation, the *chreia* cultivates the creation of meaning, investigation, and receptiveness in relation to the words of another, while at the same time cultivating the ability to connect to and develop the words of oneself. In addition, the *chreia* supports a systematic, thorough approach also available in student-driven imitation.

These dialogic exercises were accompanied with various emerging conversations on reading (Wikipedia, Harry Potter) and writing (in school, on facebook), education and institutions (turnover of teachers), democracy and justice, religion and family. Some days other residents would join us at the table, typically curious about our conversation and what we were doing. Sometimes, not mechanically, I suggested questions and feelings to be explored in writing, from journal writing to persuasive writing. I also suggested that we make posters with their poems. Only F was tempted by this idea.

These points of impact show that a group of the residents recurrently engaged in the writing workshop series in a curious and conscientious manner. Also, these points of impact signal that the workshop on some level ignited not only engagement in reading and writing, but also a wish to create, commit to, and nurture a dialogue comparable to Oldenburg's third place, the recurrent voluntary participation, the low attention to status, and the homely feel. This was reflected not only in their writing, but also in acts such as sitting still for two hours, often without a break or a smoke, making coffee, bringing biscuits, shaking hands at the end of a session, sending apologies in advance if they were unable to show up, and in the topics and nature of our conversations. Even the outbursts of anger can be seen as a wish to communicate and a sign of confidence, trust, and curiosity: "How can I dialogue if I am afraid of being displaced, the mere possibility causing me torment and weakness?" (Freire 71). These third-place traits may have been sparked or supported by the self-governed and dialogic approach of the workshop. Nevertheless, they are not an inherent consequence: the residents could have preferred to work individually with job applications and with a minimum of dialogue with regard to other matters. I came with the aim to examine whether, and to which degree, student-driven imitation could engage marginalized learners. I did not enter RG60 to manifest rules, but to come to know and match individuals and subject matter so that as many as possible could contribute (Dewey, "Experience" 56). Freire emphasizes:

> do not go to the people in order to bring them a message of "salvation", but in order to come to know through dialogue with them both their *objective situation* and their *awareness* of that situation …. One cannot expect positive results from an educational or political action program which fails to respect the particular view of the world held by the people. Such a program constitutes cultural invasion, good intentions notwithstanding. (76)

In regard to student-driven imitation, it is clear, though, that some kind of scaffolding and revised approach is needed. The residents did not bring in texts, and they apparently did not wish to repeat moves that they had already tried out. Various related dialogic exercises that supported the literate practice of student-driven imitation, on the other hand, were welcomed, including exercises that drew on their attention to publics, and exercises that trained a systematic, thorough approach to connecting reading to writing.

Student-driven Imitation and the Third Place as Potentially Transformative

Student-driven imitation draws on and combines reading and writing in community engagement. The project at RG60 based upon student-driven imitation sought a Freirean dialogue where students hold power as individual readers and writers, but neither the project nor the concept holds a collaborative problem-posing agenda, as Freire promotes (Freire 60), and as we find today in community literacy think tanks (Flower, "Public Engagement" 65). Similar to the street theater projects with homeless people facilitated by Paula Mathieu (73), student-driven imitation has a strong focus on individual expression, but then no immanent public performative dimension. Instead, the project and the concept tried to highlight entering into publics via reading, not via publishing or performance. So, relevant metaphors to describe the project are a *cultural womb,* and partly a *gate,* establishing a dialogue between people, institutions and discourses who might not otherwise meet.

The metaphor of a cultural womb implies characteristics such as nurturing, preparing, and inspiring, and the metaphor of a gate implies creating access, connections, as well as room for conflicts to unfold (Long 23). The two metaphors describe the nature and function of the third place well. This space surely has its limits. It is not the ideal public as described by Dewey: a public aroused, as a reaction to and in contrast with specific government decisions, in order to change a policy or for mutual defense (Dewey, "The Public" 27–28). Dewey described this as an ideal, aware that the complexity of modern society, especially the character of mass communication and multiple publics, is a strong constraint (126). Therefore, Dewey strongly underscores communication, the give and take of language in public and across publics in the everyday, as the ground on which a community is built and from where a public can arise (154). The third place has similar potential, but whereas communication is a practice between people everywhere, the third place is a specific space, open, neutral, and characterized by recurrent voluntary participation in dialogue and low attention to status.

The writing workshop series at RG60 based upon student-driven imitation provides insight in relation to both marginalized young people as readers and writers and the literate practice of student-driven imitation. The writing workshop series signal that young marginalized people can and wish to engage in reading and writing, including writers with a low level of formal skills as well as more experienced writers. The writing workshop series indicate that poetry can be a preferred genre for marginalized young people: a free writing space of open neutral ground, with low attention to social status; a textual third place, in which they can act independently and with confidence. Specifically in relation to student-driven imitation, the writing workshop series at RG60 discloses that this literate practice has the potential to engage and include writers of various kinds, also those on the margins. The experience reveals that this literate practice is easy to work with independently with confidence.

In addition, the writing workshop series at RG60 indicates some challenges in working with literate practice of student-driven imitation and marginalized young people: a need to provide the participants with selections of texts, a crucial need to vary exercises instead of aiming at repeating all or a selection of the dimensions, and finally, I suggest, a need for strengthening reflection and progress. With regard to variation, working more exclusively with each dimension of student-driven imitation could provide not only variation, but also a deeper understanding of each dimension, including aspects such as subject shaping, reader relation and writer's presence. Related, dialogic reading and writing exercises can also be used to support the literate practice of student-driven imitation, from Andre Breton's surreal parlor game to the classic *chreia*. Finally, I anticipate that working with journal writing could strengthen and unfold the participants' reflection in relation to central questions, such as "what fascinates me as a reader?" and "what would I like to learn?". Thus, journal writing could help explicate and maintain purposes and goals, and potentially make progress more evident.

These are the results of working with student-driven imitation in a shelter with the aim to engage young homeless people in reading and writing. This open-ended approach is one way of working with student-driven imitation. Another way is working with student-driven imitation in relation to one specific discourse or genre, which partly compromises the concept's essential property of self-governance, but opens up several scenarios, from using student-driven imitation in traditional education, in projects aimed at collaborative problem-posing in public, e.g. news paper production, to using student-driven imitation in projects aimed at reaching personal goals, e.g., job applications or dispensations, which are projects of change within reach (Cushman 13).

The residents at RG60 engaged in student-driven imitation in an open-ended manner and formed a space and dialogue around reading and writing with traits of a third place, marked by the residents' preferred genre, poetry. Oldenburg describes the third place as a place situated between home and work. Paradoxically, the residents have no home and no work. Thus, a third place may be far from what a homeless person really needs. Or maybe it is closer to it than we might think.

Works Cited

Alberti, John. "Teaching of Writing and Diversity: Access, Identity, and Achievement." *Handbook of Research on Writing*. Ed. Charles Bazerman. New York: Lawrence Erlbaum, 2008. 387–397. Print.

Asen, Robert. "A Discourse Theory of Citizenship." *Quarterly Journal of Speech* 90 (2004): 189–211. Print.

Bakhtin, Mikhail M. *The Dialogic Imagination. Four Essays*. Austin: University of Texas Press, 1981. Print.

Bender, Daniel. "Imitation." *Encyclopedia of Rhetoric and Composition. Communication from Ancient Times to the Information Age*. 1st. ed. Ed. Theresa Enos. New York: Garland, 1996. Print.

Brandt, Deborah. "Afterword. The Real and Fake Economics of Writing." *jac* 32 (2012): 769–778. Print.

Cintron, Ralph. *Angel's Town: Chero Ways, Gang Life and Rhetorics of the Everyday.* Beacon Press, 1998. Print.

———. "The Timidities of Ethnography. A Response to Bruce Horner." *jac* 22 (2002): 934–943. Print.

———. "Wearing a Pith Helmet at a Sly Angle: Or, Can Writing Researchers Do Ethnography in a Postmodern Era?" *Written Communication* 10 (1993): 371–412. Print.

Corbett, Edward P. J. "The Theory and Practice of Imitation in Classical Rhetoric." *College Composition and Communication* 22 (1971): 243–250. Print.

Cushman, Ellen. "The Rhetorician as an Agent of Social Change." *College Composition and Communication* 47 (1996): 7–28. Print.

D'Angelo, Frank J. "Imitation and Style." *College Composition and Communication* 24 (1973): 283–290. Print.

Dewey, John. *Democracy and Education, an Introduction to the Philosophy of Education.* New York: The Free Press, 1966. Print.

———. *Experience and Education.* New York: Touchstone, 1997. Print.

———. *The Public and Its Problems.* Original Publication. Athens: Swallow Press/Ohio University Press, 1927. Print.

Fish, Stanley. *How to Write a Sentence, and How to Read One.* New York: Harper, 2011. Print.

Flower, Linda. *Community Literacy and the Rhetoric of Public Engagement.* Carbondale: Southern Illinois University Press, 2008. Print.

———. "Going Public - in a Disabling Discourse." *The Public Work of Rhetoric: Citizen-Scholars and Civic Engagement.* Ed. John M. Ackerman & David J. Coogan. The University of South Carolina Press, 2010. 137–156. Print.

Freire, Paulo. *Pedagogy of the Oppressed.* Trans. Myra Bergman Ramos. London: Penguin Books, 1996. Print.

Geisler, Cheryl. "How Ought We to Understand the Concept of Rhetorical Agency?" *Rhetoric Society Quaterly* 34 (2004): 9–17. Print.

Glenn, Cheryl, Melissa A. Goldthwaite, and Robert Connors. *The St. Martin's Guide to Teaching Writing.* 5th. ed. Boston: Bedford, 2003. Print.

Hauser, Gerard. *Vernacular Voices, the Rhetoric of Publics and Public Spheres.* Columbia, University of South Carolina Press, 1999. Print.

Hoff-Clausen, Elisabeth, Christine Isager, and Lisa S. Villadsen. "Retorisk agency. Hvad skaber retorikken? [Rhetorical Agency: What Makes Rhetoric?/What Does Rhetoric Make?]." *Rhetorica Scandinavica* 33 (2005): 56–65. Print.

Huang, Hilary Bradbury. "What Is Good Action Research?" *Action Research* 8 (2010): 93–109. Print.

Kennedy, George. *Progymnasmata: Greek Textbooks of Prose, Composition, and Rhetoric.* Atlanta: Society of Biblical Literature, 2003. Print.

Lewin, Kurt. "Action Research and Minority Problems." *Journal of Social Issues* 2 (1946): 34–46. Print.
Long, Elenore. *Community Literacy and the Rhetoric of Local Publics*. West Lafayette, Indiana: Parlor Press LLC, 2008. Print.
Mathieu, Paula. *Tactics of Hope: the Public Turn in English Composition*. Portsmouth: Boynton/Cook Publishers, 2005. Print.
Matthiesen, Christina. "Elevstyret imitatio: En retorisk skrivepædagogik i teori og praksis [Student-driven imitation: A Rhetorical Writing Pedagogy in Theory and Practice]." Diss. University of Copenhagen, Copenhagen. 2013. Print.
Muckelbauer, John. "Imitation and Invention in Antiquity: A Historical-Theoretical Revision." *Rhetorica: A Journal of the History of Rhetoric* 21 (2003): 61–88. Print.
Nelson, Nancy. "The Reading-Writing Nexux in Discourse Research." *Handbook of Research on Writing*. Ed. Charles Bazerman. New York: Lawrance Erlbaum, 2008. Print.
Oldenburg, Ray. *The Great Good Place*. 2nd. edition. New York: Marlowe, 1999. Print.
Peck, Wayne Campbell, Linda Flower, and Lorraine Higgins. "Community Literacy." *Collge Composition and Communication* 46 (1995): 199–222. Print.
Quintilian. *Institutio Oratoria*. Trans. H.E. Butler. London: Harvard University Press, 1998. Print.
Rönnerman, Karin. "Action Research: Educational Tools and the Improvement of Practice." *Educational Action Research* 11 (2003): 9–21. Print.
Salvatori, Mariolina. "Reading and Writing a Text: Correlations Between Reading and Writing Patterns." *College English* 45 (1983): 657–666. Print.
Sullivan, Dale. "Attitudes Toward Imitation: Classical Culture and the Modern Temper." *Rhetoric Review* 8 (1989): 5–21. Print.
Terrill, Robert. "Mimesis, Duality, and Rhetorical Education." *Rhetoric Society Quarterly* 41 (2011): 295–315. Print.
Warner, Michael. *Publics and Counterpublics*. New York: Zone Books, 2005. Print.
———. "Publics and Counterpublics (abbreviated version)." *Quarterly Journal of Speech* 88 (2002): 413–425. Print.
Warnick, Bryan R. *Imitation and Education: A Philosophical Inquiry into Learning by Example*. Albany: State University of New York Press, 2008. Print. SUNY Series, The Philosophy of Education.

Author Bio

Christina Matthiesen is an assistant professor at Aarhus University, Department of Education, in Denmark. She holds a MA and PhD in rhetoric from the University of Copenhagen, where she taught writing and theories of rhetoric and composition pedagogy from 2002-2012. In her dissertation from 2013 she introduces and investigates the concept and literate practice of student-driven imitation, reinvigorating Quintilian's progressive notion of imitation. She would like to give her thanks to Linda Flower for her invaluable assistance in the development of this essay.

Community Engagement in a Graduate-Level Community Literacy Course

Lauren Marshall Bowen, Kirsti Arko, Joel Beatty, Cindy Delaney, Isidore Dorpenyo, Laura Moeller, Elsa Roberts, and John Velat

A case study of a graduate-level community literacy seminar that involved a tutoring project with adult digital literacy learners, this essay illustrates the value of community outreach and service-learning for graduate students in writing studies. Presenting multiple perspectives through critical reflection, student authors describe how their experiences contextualized, enhanced, and complicated their theoretical knowledge of public rhetoric and community literacy. Inspired by her students' reflections, the faculty co-author issues a call to graduate programs in writing, rhetoric, literacy studies, and technical communication to develop a conscious commitment to graduate students' civic engagement by supporting opportunities to learn, teach, and research with community partners.

Introduction (Lauren)

In the spring of 2014, my co-authors and I met for a Community Literacy seminar in the Rhetoric and Technical Communication graduate program (now retitled: "Rhetoric, Theory, and Culture") at Michigan Technological University. Part of the course required students to volunteer as tutors and ethnographic observers during the Breaking Digital Barriers project: a free digital literacy assistance program organized by university faculty and students for members of the local community. It didn't take long for us to encounter the uncomfortable contradictions inherent in community-based research and pedagogies. As Figure 1 below demonstrates, we concentrated on pulling at the tangled strands of civic engagement in higher education, wherein the goal of "critical consciousness" is entwined with the marketability ("$") of a university and its graduates.

Our struggle was underscored by the realization that community literacy studies—despite its major growth in the past two decades—remains at the fringes of the academy. Students commented with some regularity that, even within a graduate program with strong commitments to off-campus partnerships and critical consciousness, they had not yet taken a graduate course that actually led them off campus or focused so explicitly on *action*. This observation describes a fundamental challenge in many graduate programs in writing studies and related fields: the incentive to recognize rhetoric and

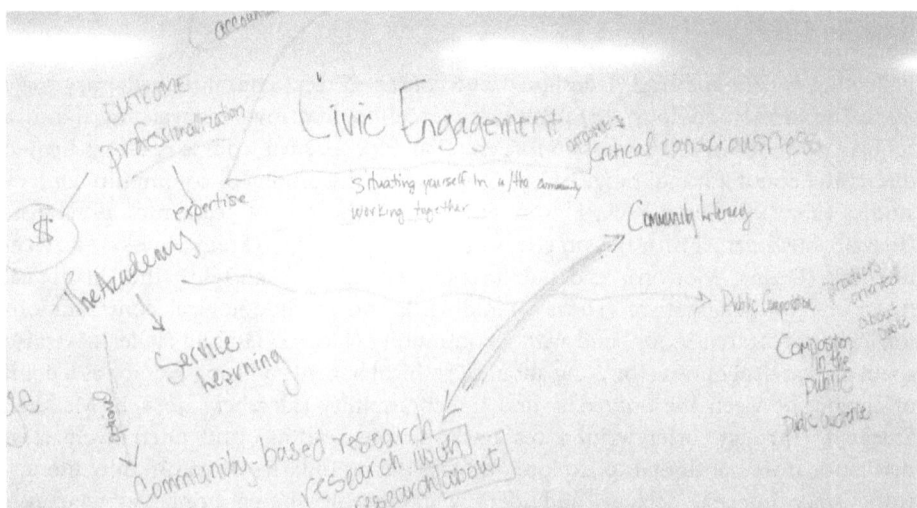

Figure 1: Writing on the board from a student-led class discussion. Photo by Lauren Bowen.

literacy as situated, public, social, and political domains of activity is at odds with the persistent belief that academic success requires a focus on activities removed from civic life.

In this essay, my co-authors and I present a case study of our community literacy seminar so that we might articulate some of the outcomes of a deliberate integration of community outreach in graduate-level scholarship and research. In a sense, this essay contributes to a conversation begun in the pages of this journal in 2008, when Ellen Cushman, Jeffrey Grabill, and five graduate students reflected on their efforts to trace theories, methodologies, and pedagogies associated with community literacy studies (Fero, et al.). In planning for the community literacy course at Michigan Tech, I was particularly mindful of Cushman and Grabill's ultimate concern that, without a community outreach project, the graduate seminar seemed "too conceptual" and could not examine "the tension between our often elegant theories of what communities are, what literacy should be, and how we ought to design our activities and the less-than-ideal realities of literacy projects" (90).

In response to this concern, I looked to the Breaking Digital Barriers project (for which I was already a volunteer) as a site for action and critical reflection, reminiscent of Freire's *praxis*. Our weekly experiences with the community project led to productive examinations of the tensions between theory and practice in community literacy studies. Following a bit of context for the community literacy seminar and the Breaking Digital Barriers project, this essay presents my co-authors' critical reflections of their experiences as graduate students/teachers/researchers, in which they identify the outcomes of the community outreach experience in relation to their own goals as intellectuals, teachers, activists, and community members.

Background (Lauren)

Following Cushman's lead, I designed our course to treat community literacy as "a discipline, a methodology, an institutional location that involves teaching, [and] a scholarly or administrative mission" (Fero et al. 90). As such, course readings invited discussion about a broad range of issues, including the origins of community literacy studies (Howard; Long; Peck, Flower, & Higgins); the role of academics as activists (Bizzell; Cushman; Fish); the practices of critical pedagogy (Freire; hooks), service-learning (Deans; Morton), and public composition (Fleckenstein); the theoretical framework of pragmatism (Dewey; Goldblatt); and methodological considerations for literacy research in, on, and with a community (Flower; Grabill; Heller). We also spent a great deal of time thinking about the ethical hazards of using literacy as a point of contact between the university and the community (Herzberg; Joseph; Mathieu; Stuckey). Through brief written responses to the readings and often lively class discussions, we continued to explore and test the boundaries of community literacy work, trace internal debates, and identify commonly shared principles whenever possible.

Our thinking about these readings was filtered through our work with the Breaking Digital Barriers project (or BDB). Founded in 2011 by Dr. Charles Wallace, an associate professor in computer science at Michigan Tech, Breaking Digital Barriers is a volunteer-based outreach project that supports the development of digital literacies in the communities surrounding the university. A beautiful, historic area, Houghton County's particular living conditions present many challenges for residents. Breaking Digital Barriers responds to a need that is exacerbated by three particular conditions of life in Houghton:

- **It is remote.** Hundreds of miles from any major cities, Houghton sits on the rugged Keweenaw Peninsula on Lake Superior, whose "lake effect" brings more than 200 inches of snow each year. The lengthy, snowy winters make travel on the area's few major roadways a dangerous prospect for most of the year. Further, the population density of Houghton County is low, at about 36 people per square mile of dry land (U.S. Census Bureau, Gazetteer Files), which is comparable to the density of Kansas or Utah (U.S. Census Bureau, Statistical Abstracts). (In Keweenaw County, just a few miles up the road, the population drops to a mere four people per square mile.)

- **It is relatively poor.** Once a booming copper mining community, the area has faced a major economic shift since mining halted in the mid-20th century. During the BDB's first year of operation, Houghton County recorded a jobless rate of 9.6% (Michigan Department of Technology, Labor, and Budget). According to census estimates, nearly a quarter of its residents had incomes below the poverty level, while the per capita income in the city of Houghton hovered just over $15,000—not quite half the per capita income of the United States as a whole (U.S. Census, American Community Survey). In contrast, the average salary of an individual Michigan Tech employee was $51,000 (Michigan Technological University), and the average undergraduate could expect to earn $1,000 more during their first year on the job than the average Houghton County *household* would have earned in the same year (Michigan Tech Career Services; U.S. Census, American Community Survey).

- **It is aging.** Like the rest of the United States, the population of older adults in Michigan is increasing at a rapid rate (Day). Meanwhile, in 2012 more young, college-educated individuals migrated out of than into the State of Michigan (Gimarc). Again, like most of the country, older adults in Houghton County find younger relatives moving greater distances away.

This triple threat makes for an especially dire situation for elder adults in the Houghton area, who have been increasingly dependent upon digital networks to connect with the world from their isolated homes, and whose resources for accessing and learning to navigate technologies are set back by economic limitations and the exodus of younger relatives and friends.

The BDB project sought to intervene in the growing problem of elder isolation by supporting older adults' digital literacy development, including critical literacies (Banks; Selber). The project is primarily run by university volunteers who offer free, one-on-one computer tutorials for local adults, typically over age 50. Although the group has expanded its reach as additional needs are identified (e.g., in assisted living facilities and employment agencies), the core of the project involves weekly tutorial sessions held during the academic calendar year. For one hour each Friday morning at the local public library, volunteer faculty and students from Michigan Tech answer questions, provide moral support, and help learners walk through various tasks involving digital technologies. Questions from learners often focus on issues of function, such as how to write an email. Often these questions lead to critical discussions of technologies and the roles that they play, or do not play, in learners' lives.

As attendance at BDB sessions continues to climb, the project's central challenge is sustainability. In part to address the need for consistent volunteer participation, I required graduate students to work as participant-observers of BDB tutorial sessions that semester. Working in pairs, students split their time between assisting learners with their individual questions and taking field notes of the interactions between tutors and learners. The observations served as a form of community needs assessment, which would otherwise have been difficult to elicit directly from the rotating cast of community members with an enormous range of interests and experience. This observation-based needs assessment ultimately led to a pedagogical application, as the students developed and facilitated a series of free public workshops: a workshop on internet safety practices, such as spam recognition and password protection; a workshop on digital photo file management strategies; and a collaborative learning workshop for building women's knowledge and confidence in using digital technology.

In what follows, these master's and doctoral students discuss the learning outcomes of their experiences with the BDB project with particular attention to how those experiences have impacted their relationship with the field of community literacy studies[1]. These students entered the classroom with various cultural and national backgrounds; different disciplinary perspectives, including technical communication, literacy studies, writing center theory, philosophy, and gender studies; a wide range of personal and professional histories with teaching, community organizing, and activism; and a widely varied sense of how community literacy studies might (or might not) factor into their careers in academia and beyond.

Critical Reflections on Community Literacy and Breaking Digital Barriers

The Value of Reciprocity: Learning Through Hands-On Experience (Cindy)

As a part of the Community Literacy class, the Breaking Digital Barriers project reinforced for me the importance of moving students outside of academia and engaging with people in the community. The project gave each of us a chance to engage in a hands-on experience (an approach I'd never experienced before) and reinforced my understanding of the importance of reciprocity, a fair "give-and-take" (Cushman 16) relationship that benefits both the members of the academy and the community through "the long process of self disclosure and listening... [and] identify[ing] with each other" (18). Although I worked as an undergraduate student consultant at my college writing center for two years, I was nervous to work with older adults, and I was unsure of what they could gain from my limited understanding of the potential technologies and processes that they could bring to the library. As we worked through the course, my initial hesitation subsided as my classmates and I learned the importance of working as a support system for the session attendees and sharing in their discoveries. Instead of misunderstanding my role as a consultant as the teacher who bestows expertise upon the student, I would be sharing expertise and learning from the participants in a way that benefited us both.

By working with the Houghton community outside of Michigan Tech, the members of the class bridged the gap between the university and the session attendees by operating as a face-to-face support group, sharing their own knowledge and stories of working and experimenting with technologies, encouraging more technological curiosity by working through issues together, and bringing "technological training to those with limited access [and resources, including support systems]" (McKee and Blair 34). John, Isidore, and I continually worked with a couple named Fred and Elizabeth throughout our time with Breaking Digital Barriers. Based on our interactions with Fred[2] and Elizabeth, I began to note the importance of occasionally stepping out of tutoring to talk about life "offline," often sharing stories beyond the purpose of learning about new technologies. I believe that the couple continually returned to work with us because we would discuss our lives outside of the technology we were using or reflect on how it enhanced the world around us. For example, during one of our sessions, John and Fred held a longer discussion about Houghton, hunting, and how the iPad could enhance the experience of hunters in general. By sharing a mutual interest, John developed a way to bridge the age gap between himself and Fred and showed that, while Fred's expertise at that moment existed outside of technology, John could learn something from Fred as well.

Our experience with Fred and Elizabeth demonstrated to us that, even though our work with the Breaking Digital Barriers sessions was "initiated [as a class project] within the institution and extend[ed] outward" (Mathieu 111), it contributed a genuine sense of reciprocity throughout the semester. While the session and workshop attendees were given the chance to engage their technological curiosities, build their knowledge about their devices, and receive one-on-one support from the class members, my classmates and I were given the chance to engage some of the principles and concepts discussed in class readings and see how they operated in action and outside of the academy. As the measure of the effectiveness of my group's support and assistance, we contributed to the technological literacies of a couple who began to feel more at ease with operating their iPad, what Fred called their new "toy," even as we tutors became increasingly comfortable in our own personal use of technologies.

Over time, Fred (the primary operator of the iPad) and I both became less afraid of experimenting with the device and realized that we could collaboratively resolve issues that would arise. He also began to realize the extent of the possibilities for communicating with his family members through other applications such as FaceTime, reminders, notes, the camera, and so on. During our final session together, Fred brought in a brand new iPhone (an anniversary gift from Elizabeth) and we began setting up his voicemail. When I noted their investment in another Apple product, Elizabeth commented that, after all of our sessions together, Fred felt so comfortable with the iPad that they decided to buy the phone. Moreover, I began to appreciate these applications as an iPhone/MacBook user, since I use a majority of them to enhance my own time management as a graduate student and even keep up my social relationships. Through consistency and encouragement, Fred, Elizabeth, and our group members achieved reciprocity by contributing to each other's familiarity with technology by fostering a sense of comfortable support and experimentation with their "toys."

Problem-solving Rhetors (Isidore)

I enrolled in the class because of my interest in rhetoric and my desire to explore how rhetorical theories can help me understand rhetoric not in a negative way, but as a problem-solving mechanism. More important, I wanted to understand what the "public turn" of rhetoric meant. I was very delighted when readings from such scholars as Linda Flower, Ellen Cushman, Jeffrey Grabill, Keith Morton, and several other scholars hinted that, as rhetors, we are social agents and we can initiate changes in our communities. How exactly can we do that? This sense of applying rhetorical theories to effect changes in our communities became more relevant to me when we embarked on a semester-long, practice-oriented project that engaged directly with a local community.

Toward the end of the semester, we were asked to design workshops for clients who attended our tutoring sessions. Each group sifted through weekly written observations to find out the most pressing needs of BDB participants. My group observed that participants wanted to learn how to take and edit digital photos, to learn how to transfer photos from camera to computers, to know more about email, to figure out how to recognize and organize icons, how to use Skype, and (overwhelmingly) how to keep track of passwords. Based on our experiences we decided to settle on one of the pressing issues that confronted us: how do people stay safe on the internet? With more than ten people attending our workshop, it became apparent that people were interested in knowing more about internet scams and frauds.

Our internet safety workshop threw more light on an issue raised by Peck, Flower, and Higgins, who describe the community center as a forum for people to begin a broader conversation about issues they care most about (200). For us and our participants, the BDB tutoring project became a space to discuss issues of concern. The workshop was not unidirectional; that is, it was not a medium of knowledge transfer from us ("experts") to them ("non-experts"). It was a moment of exploration and discovery for both tutors and participants. We had participants ask a lot of questions. Some shared their experiences. I observed the level of seriousness that participants attached to the workshop. Participants were hungry for more; they were ready and willing to participate. I saw what it meant to be a member of a community. We had the same purpose, the same goal. The workshop was scheduled to end at 10:00am, but we continued and participants were ready and willing to stay.

The workshop also strengthened the argument that community literacy provides a site of rhetorical intervention. Thus, we started our inquiry into the community through weekly tutorials and observations. The conversations we had with people and the field notes we took gave us enough insights into the issues our participants were faced with. We organized the workshop in order to help participants understand and know how to stay safe on the internet, intervening based on inquiry and information gathering. In essence, we reflected and took action.

Belonging to a community forms a quintessential aspect of community literacy scholarship and pedagogy. The local public becomes an important "object of inquiry and a site for rhetorical intervention" (Long 25). More importantly, the local public becomes a site for rhetorical engagement and relationship building. It inspires an "ethic of love and justice," "hope," a "love ethic," and "reciprocal relations," and it becomes a standard "for ethical action in the research paradigm to facilitate social change" (qtd. in Long 25). The emphasis on local public works to "dismantle university/'white' privilege and to reconfigure writing instruction outside the academic classroom..." (Long 26). It is a means of speaking *about* and *for* silenced voices, or a moment of engaging *with* difference. Community literacy, Flower makes us aware, "is a rhetorical practice for inquiry and social change" (6). In her estimation, community literacy is not solely focused on language of urban "others." Neither is it a vehicle for academicians to talk about others. It is "an intercultural dialogue *with others* on issues that *they* identify as sites of struggles" (Flower 19). It enables faculty and college students to start solving problems in a community.

The "public turn" of rhetoric moves rhetors from their ivory towers on university campuses to the communities around them. It helps us to bridge the age-old binary between theory and practice. We bring theory to practice and practice to theory in service of our communities. We become agents of change. The "public turn" of rhetoric is not only interested in academic conversations, it gives rhetors the tools to apply practical judgment (*phronesis*) to solving community problems. We are ambassadors of change. Reflection and social action are the core tenets of community literacy and rhetoric. The public turn, for me, becomes a moment of engagement with the community around us in order to explore issues of concern and a moment of helping one another in order to solve complex problems. Rhetoric becomes the medium of exploration and a tool for inquiry.

The Pragmatics of Transformational Projects (Elsa)

The roots of community literacy programs can be traced to community centers, such as Hull House, that developed at the turn of the century in response to the need for educational and recreational facilities for immigrant and lower income people in urban areas. From the very beginning, community literacy has blended idealism and pragmatism with varying levels of success. The discipline's tendency toward self-reflection seems to work as a tempering mechanism that has kept the focus of community literacy on a pragmatic course that doesn't lose sight of its larger goal (social transformation). Concern for this can be seen in the work of Peck, Flower, and Higgins, who speak of wrestling against "[r]esearch agendas, framed in the armchair of theory and untested in the context of real people and problems" (219), a perspective pointedly echoed by Linda Flower in *Community Literacy and the Rhetoric of Public Engagement*, where she continues to refine her approach to effective community literacy. Another carefully considered aspect of the field is the motivation behind academics' participation in community literacy programs. Scholars such as Morton and Mathieu emphasize the importance of developing a relationship with one's local community as a necessary step in any authentic project that purports to be *for* a community.

My work with Breaking Digital Barriers indicated to me that BDB was a project that grew into being in response to a community need and desire. Working on a community literacy project while engaging with academic texts on community literacy reinforced the theoretical basis of the field and demonstrated to me how theory and practice can be intertwined in a reciprocal relationship. Participation in BDB was an expression of an aspect of what we were learning in class and hence stayed true to the ethics of community literacy, which emphasize practice in relationship to theory, as well as the ethical obligation of academics to go beyond the university. Although not the goal, in working with participants at BDB, I developed a deeper appreciation for what I was learning, as I put what were formerly theoretical concepts and pedagogical approaches into practice. But an almost paradoxical part of that appreciation was the realization that what is learned in the classroom does not translate neatly into the field. Tutoring people at the BDB sessions prevented me from becoming overly idealistic about literacy; for example, one of the women I worked with just wanted to buy maps for an upcoming trip. She didn't appear to be interested in digital literacy beyond achieving a simple, transactional goal, and she was far from the only participant with whom this was the case. Often I found that a user's interest was limited to one of functional literacy. This aptly demonstrated to me the very constraints of theory that community literacy scholars so frequently detail.

Because of this experience, I was able to reflect more critically on community literacy as described by authors like Linda Flower and Eli Goldblatt and consider how their work might actually translate in a community different from the ones in which they worked. For example, Flower strives to maintain a careful balance between pragmatism and idealism—a thread that runs throughout her book. Her idealism is most evident in the stories she chooses to highlight of participants engaging civic activism through her project of intercultural inquiry; for example, Flower describes the efforts of 13-year-old Shirley to commit to paper her experiences with racialized police harassment. In the excerpt Flower provides, Shirley creates an essay that is included in a group publication called *Listen Up! Teen Stress*. This document, designed for intra and inter public engagement is then the source of a public reading attended by public officials. The implication is that such inspiring stories will result in community change, perhaps even transformation; but the question remains, what is the tangible result? Has racial profiling been diminished, for example?

Upon working in the everyday context of the BDB, without the lens of time to pick out the most inspirational stories, I became more skeptical of stories of individual social transformation. What I observed indicated that most users were not intentionally seeking out a program like BDB for that purpose. Rather, participants generally had what most would consider mundane goals, such as learning more about features of Facebook, how to use the new Surface tablet interface, and searching for a place to purchase a paper map. There is no need to diminish the importance of functional literacy, of mundane objectives in contributing to the loftier goals scholar-activists typically envision. In fact, in community literacy projects, including Flower's, and also those described by Cushman, Herzberg, and Grabill, one of the grounding factors in developing a program is that it sprang from the everyday needs of the people, or as Goldblatt puts it, from self-interest. Breaking Digital Barriers did this as well; it functioned to meet needs individuals in the community had and people were drawn to participate in it due to self-interest (the desire to use computers for their own purposes).

Although overall the field of community literacy has worked diligently to curb theoretical idealism, it still tends to surface in the stories and examples researchers pull from their work. This has a very natural cause, the desire to demonstrate that one's program is working and, more importantly, that there is evidence of more transformational change than mundane stories would seem to tell. It is also how one continues to receive funding and support. Ironically, it may be pragmatism, in some respects, that feeds such idealism. It is only in continually returning to what grounds this field, projects, that theoretical idealism can be tempered by everyday experience. The practicality that this engenders is, I believe, vital for community literacy as a field and a practice to continue transforming theory, pedagogy, and method into something tangible, fallible, and perhaps most importantly, malleable.

The Ethical Contingencies of Sharing (and Not Sharing) Knowledge (Joel)

In this section I recount my interactions with Sally, a middle-aged BDB participant whose dependence on social support networks in her technological literacy practices revealed to me a crucial ethical challenge inherent in community literacy work. Unemployed for a number of years, Sally was determined to learn the skills she needed to apply for jobs online. I was eager to help Sally from the beginning. But over the months I spent working with her, I learned that helping *someone* in the community literacy program context really means helping *someone in a particular situation*. My work with Sally has complicated for me the ethics of acting as an expert—that moment when, as Linda Flower cautions, "well meaning volunteerism" can turn community practitioners into knowledge servers (103).

Sally initially came to the BDB sessions because she needed assistance with her résumé and submitting online job applications. However, she had a rather inefficient process of preparing her résumé digitally. She lived with her sister and had access to a home computer, but said her sister wasn't very helpful in explaining how the computer worked, and continually warned Sally that her personal information might be "stolen" if she sent her résumé via email. Sally explained that technical problems made her sister nervous about Sally using the computer at all, and so technical issues would remain unresolved. To avoid adding to her sister's anxiety and risking her access to the computer, Sally would print out her résumé and other documents and mail the hard copies to her friend Jim, who lived out of state. Jim would then digitize the documents and send the files back to her via email—messages she would sometimes "lose" in an email account hosted under her sister's home ISP account, which was occasionally rendered inaccessible when Sally's sister changed its password. When her access to email was interrupted, Sally tended to blame herself—a tendency partly explained by Sally's eventual disclosure that she had a severe learning disability. Over time, she had come to see herself as the problem.

It took me a few weeks to assess Sally's system of communication, but I felt that, alongside Sally's sister and her friend Jim, I was also playing a mediating role among Sally's goals, her positive and negative experiences with technology, and the supporting people around her. At one point, I wanted to suggest that Sally create a separate email address, such as a Gmail account, that would be much easier to access and maintain on her own. It would also give her a stable place to store her digital files and exchange documents with Jim, and it would bypass her sister's gatekeeping. But in considering ways to streamline the communication process in Sally's job search, I felt the need to consider her overall situation, including those relationships that would be there well after our BDB sessions were over. Setting up a Gmail account for Sally would have been easy enough for me to do. However, given her reliance on her sister's help (which likely extended beyond her technological needs), this might have compounded Sally's fears and anxieties surrounding the internet and other technologies.

This situation marked the potential for me and the BDB project "to replicate the social structures that are part of the problem," as a result of pairing an "expert" with a "client, patient, or the educationally deficient" (Flower 103). To resist this tendency,

Flower suggests that the "knowledge expert" repeatedly ask two important questions: "Who am I? What am I doing here?" (101). I found Flower's suggestion to maintain the spirit of inquiry vital to my interactions with Sally which, from the first, were laden with potential to make her situation worse by knowledge-serving without regard to the specifics of Sally's situation.

Ultimately, I decided against helping Sally create a Gmail account. On one hand, a Gmail account would eliminate many of her frustrations regarding access to her email and might have given her much more autonomy over her online communications. On the other hand, Sally relied on others to help her when things went wrong. I didn't feel it was my place as a transitory member of her technical support network to disrupt or complicate more permanent relationships. Plus, she had the support of her friend Jim, as well as limited access to a home computer via a reluctant sister.

As I wrote my reflections on my experiences with Sally, I experienced feelings of culpability and responsibility about the information I was giving her. I didn't think Sally couldn't manage a Gmail account on her own, given her disability and difficulties with memory. Instead, I thought that a Gmail account would cause ripples of anxiety and tension in Sally's existing support networks. In one of our last sessions, Sally said the most striking thing to me while waiting for the slow library internet connection to load a webpage. I said, "It just takes time with these things sometimes," and Sally said, "Time is all I have." I couldn't help but feel a bit sad after hearing that. All Sally wanted was to work a part-time job. I found myself more than willing to lend whatever "expertise" I had to help her apply for jobs and work on computer skills, but I knew, too, that I had to do so without intruding on or jeopardizing her precarious access to technology at home.

Thinking about Sustainability (John)

I came to the Breaking Digital Barriers project (BDB) with over twenty years of domestic and overseas experience in technical assistance and capacity building (most recently providing technical assistance to American Indian communities throughout the midwestern and eastern U.S.), hoping to improve on personal experience through theory and academically influenced practice. I have always been troubled by the potential to wreak havoc when a humanitarian aid bomb is dropped in a community, and was looking to academia to help avoid the typical pitfalls of community aid and support projects that can alienate beneficiaries, make them dependent, or fail to provide sustained benefit. The BDB experience ended up reinforcing both the positive and negative experiences of community service, but it also provided me with new perspectives on how to avoid the negatives.

The BDB program provided patrons with eager, young volunteers who brought the knowledge and resources to solve all the computer and information technology problems an isolated retiree could ever face—or at least that was part of the expectation from both sides. When we, the BDB activists, visited a local assisted-living home for a single one-hour tutoring session, we offered plenty of knowledge and energy, but we probably provided more friendly conversation than effective assistance with computer problems. It's not easy to unravel a novice's Facebook, Skype, and Apple Store credentials in fifty minutes, so posting a single photo turned into more frustration with already frustrating devices than any kind of knowledge transfer. At both the assisted-living home and the library, when we could not resolve issues with passwords, digital rights management, and access rights, clients gave up on those tasks and said, "Nevermind, I don't need to do that anyway." These experiences reminded me that, without a sustained and deliberate effort to guide community participants along a path of learning, the effort can alienate a new computer user to the whole concept of powerful and beneficial technology, and consequently undermine future efforts of others seeking to collaborate with community members.

Creating sustainable community service programs is a challenge, particularly when the providers are busy graduate students committing a semester to the program. Whether the services are provided by a well-funded philanthropic organization or students in a graduate class, all service programs face the limits of staff availability and project end dates. The ideal community service program will therefore seek to overcome these limitations by transferring skills and resources to the local recipients, providing for a self-sustaining program that continues to meet local needs long after the students have completed their final papers, the sponsors have moved on, or the project has run out of money. To reach this ideal, service programs should foster communities that build local capacity and intertwine the benefactors with the recipients, benefitting all parties involved and making the whole process more effective.

While the BDB portion of our graduate class did not initially emphasize community and capacity building, the potential developed through the existence of the program in a public library with regular patrons from a small community. The program's close association with dedicated faculty, students, and staff from the local university also contributed to community development across the academic/non-academic community divide. In many cases, those assisting bring vast knowledge and financial resources to bear, and it is easy for the recipients to subjugate themselves to a beneficiary role that requires little more than gratitude to keep resource contributions flowing. Morton identified this problem of power differential in a university setting:

> From a critical perspective, the experts necessary to design and manage a program magnify inequalities of power, and make the served dependent on the expert. This is a particularly dangerous trap for colleges and universities which are generally regarded as repositories of expertise, and employ research tools that non-experts cannot master. (22)

The development of a community of patrons and providers helped diffuse the potential disruption of resource surges, and also helped overcome the power differential between benefactor and beneficiary.

Seeking to create a sustainable, effective program has its own perils. Paula Mathieu warns us about seeking sustainability for its own sake, which can predetermine the kind of program that we create (99). As a program built upon the time, energy, and eagerness of university faculty and students, the BDB risks falling into this trap of predetermining the type of program offered and seeking sustainability over meeting evolving community needs. Compounding this risk, the tutors were students with varying technical and pedagogical skills who had to learn to be effective tutors and complete their own assignments within a ten-week schedule, further leading us down a potential path of determinism. So, while we repeated some of the mistakes Mathieu warned us about, we also did as Thomas Deans suggests in "Sustainability Deferred": we did our best and moved on.

The limitations of community service programs, particularly the volunteer or compelled-volunteering types like BDB, do not prevent me from undertaking these types of projects. Building sustainable, intertwined communities helps mitigate limitations; the more severely resource-limited programs sometimes require closer ties between benefactor and beneficiary, which can be less disruptive than and just as beneficial as well-funded programs with expert humanitarian aid commandos. To BDB's benefit, the organizers' and tutors' lives are at least temporarily intertwined with the community. As with Deans, Grabill, and McKee and Blair, we live in this community, and, for better or worse, we will make mistakes, learn from them, and learn from each other.

Witnessing and Responding to the Digital Divide (Kirsti and Laura)

In their article on community-based technological literacy programs for older adults, Heidi McKee and Kristine Blair quote the following statement from Rachel, one of their workshop participants:

> It's a psychological thing when an older person—and it doesn't happen with young people because they grow up with computers—when you look at the computer you just feel totally overwhelmed, like this thing is some kind of monster. It's got all these wires and god only knows what's going to happen. We have, I guess, a little bit of a fear like – I hate to say this, but even for women, especially, you know because it was just a totally different society… I mean people thought differently about what women should be doing and what they shouldn't. (25)

Rachel identifies two factors that, in her experience, cause what she refers to as "psychological" barriers when dealing with technology: age and gender. On the one hand, she feels that her generation is at a disadvantage due to a lack of exposure to technology. On the other hand, she has the impression that traditional gender roles impact women of her generation more strongly than younger women.

Rachel's statement summarizes the overall impression that we gained during the Breaking Digital Barriers project. In our tutorial sessions, we predominantly worked with women, and a clear theme arose throughout the course of the project: a lack of confidence and agency with technology and the tendency to rely heavily on a male member of the family (husbands, sons, nephews). In one of our sessions with a couple, we asked the woman if she would like to join us at the table to participate in the session. She said, "No, thank you. He'll learn from you, and then he can teach me later at home." Similarly, another woman lacked any of the necessary information for her accounts or passwords: "He does all of that," she explained, referring to her husband. This lack of agency and access even led to extreme self-doubt and criticism: "I'm so stupid with this" was only one of the self-derogatory statements we heard from women expressing their relation to technology. When asked about which technologies *she* used and owned, one woman shared her technological literacy history only using the pronoun "we," again referring to herself and her husband. However, as we expected, all of these women were no less able to deal with technology than any of the male participants.

Access to and the ability to make use of technology are determined by a broad variety of factors. Yet it is our impression that specifically when dealing with older adults, little attention has been paid to the fact that older adults comprise a highly heterogeneous group. Our participants were mainly white and often well-educated; the gender gap we discovered may be but one additional factor. We decided to take a step in bridging the gap by offering *A Women's Technology Workshop* to help women become more confident with technology. When responding to a question regarding her technological confidence in the workshop, one of our participants echoed Rachel's statement when she said, "I don't want to be a sexist, but men tend to be much more assertive, and they tend to interrupt you." A common theme amongst this group pointed to the lack of space that women have to assert themselves when it comes to technology. Yet when one of us (Laura) attempted to find empirical data that would confirm our theory of an age-*gender*-divide, she came across results that were somewhat surprising. The most recent study on the digital divide was the Pew Research Center's Internet Project on technology and old age, which used data from 2013 (Smith). While the data confirms a gap between male and female users above the age of 65, the extensive report on the study does not mention the gender divide at all. It seemed that despite the differences we noticed amongst genders in this age bracket, no one is paying close attention. There seems to be more to the story than what is being told.

The technology workshop that we offered was meant to do something about this gender divide that we had witnessed week after week. Among others, the works of Linda Flower, Caroline Heller, bell hooks, and Paulo Freire were particularly influential. The workshop began and ended in guided conversations based on one of Peck, Flower, and Higgins' four key aims for community literacy, intercultural conversation. "[C]ommunity literacy," they argue, "expands the table by bringing into conversation multiple and often unheard perspectives" (205). All participants, including ourselves, shared personal experience, prior knowledge, and challenges with technologies. The value of these conversations came not only from the varied perspectives, but also in the value of *being heard* as a form of empowerment. As quoted by Heller, Tenderloin Reflection and Education Center director Ben Clarke points out that to "take action and challenge those circumstances [...] happens through being heard" (7-8). Though we cannot say for sure, these women may have never been given a space to talk about their technological strengths and the value of their prior knowledge, even if it dated back to the 70s. Also inspired by Freire's critique of the "banking concept of education," we attempted to break down any hierarchies. After hearing about both their needs and their prior knowledge, we formed groups. We joined the groups not as teachers, but as participants. For instance, while working in a team with a participant on her iPad, Laura highlighted that she had no experience with Apple products and that she was improvising. The participant later wrote in a reflection: "I can't know it all, just keep pecking away." While acting as a participant and not the teacher, Laura was able to lessen the hierarchy and admit that she too was still learning, serving as a perfect example of how technology forces all users to continue to learn in order to keep up, even for someone who may seem to be the expert.

Flower specifically talks of community literacy's effect on the individuals to "return to their own spheres enabled to think and act differently in ways appropriate to their situation" (29). It was our goal that when these women left the workshop, they may feel a small sense of empowerment and more confidence to speak up about the skills they did have, to try new things without fear of looking stupid, and to take back some of their agency. Flower understands rhetorical agency as the "work of *everyday people*" (206). That is how we understood ourselves: a small group of everyday people having a conversation. On the surface this may seem powerless, but that was hardly the case, as we were assured through our course readings and discussions. Being able to move from theory to action is the formula that made this course so valuable. Seldom, if ever, are graduate students given this opportunity during their coursework, yet it not only enhanced what we offered to the workshop participants but also provided us the chance to put the theory into practice. Only when we were able to take community literacy into the community did it impact both ourselves and others. To us, a statement often attributed to Margaret Mead captures it best: "Never doubt that a small group of thoughtful, committed individuals can change the world. Indeed it's the only thing that ever has."

Conclusion (Lauren)

As my co-authors demonstrate above, the turn toward community engagement can catalyze important aspects of graduate education in writing studies. In some instances, the project was an important means of extending (not just applying) classroom-based learning, as evidenced by Cindy's contextualized understanding of reciprocity, and by Isidore's defining of rhetoric in terms of "problem-solving" and action, rather than seeing rhetoric "in a negative way." At the same time, the BDB project also occasioned critique of the readings and theories we encountered in the classroom. Elsa and Joel in particular call attention to the messiness and tension so often elided in published accounts of community engagement, and remind us to ask: What "violence" can literacy work do? In addition to the refraction of classroom learning, the BDB project also appears to have been a site for re-visioning action and engagement. As John, Laura, and Kirsti recount moving from theory to action (and back again), their facility with social critique serves as an important critical lens for the existing practices of the BDB project and for future community literacy efforts.

To follow my co-authors' astute reflections with some parting comments of my own, I offer a critical reflection on *their* observations and raise two particular points of concern, which I will suggest are different indicators of the same problem. First, as is captured in the reflections above, my co-authors universally note that the outreach experience called sharp attention to their positionality as academics in a literacy-oriented community setting. As a group, we were critical of the "logic of expertise" (Flower 105) with which the BDB operates, and worked to resist that logic. I am not altogether surprised by their sensitivity to expert/novice or professional/client relationships with community members. After all, one of their primary objectives as graduate students is to develop expertise in a given field, even as they enter a scene in which that aspirational identity of "expert" is simultaneously challenged and reified.

Second, as I noted in the introduction, my co-authors were quick to point out during class that, despite their interest in community literacy and action, our engagement project was a one-off experience. Some have continued working with the BDB alongside other volunteer tutors, but most do not have the time or energy—circumstances for which I have a great deal of sympathy. Most will not again have a built-in opportunity for civic engagement in their classes, and nothing in their degree requirements suggests they should seek such opportunities on their own. And, unless one of my colleagues elects to teach a similar course, it will be several years before something like Community Literacy will be made available to other RTC students. As evidenced in my co-authors' reflections, our class offered students many benefits of learning through engagement, and it supported a much-needed relationship between university and community. But then the class ended, and with it, students' clearest (if imperfect) source of support for community engagement.

My co-authors' sensitivity to their roles as literacy and technology experts and the unsustainable role of civic engagement in their graduate degree programs are intertwined concerns that prevail in many graduate programs in writing studies. Since writing studies' "public turn" (Mathieu), graduate students are increasingly drawn toward community engagement and public scholarship. However, these same students quickly encounter conflicting messages. Faced with warnings that such work would be considered a diversion from professional activities that *actually* count, graduate students are bewildered by a compelling call that, alas, must not be answered before tenure. In a *Reflections* special issue on this very problem, Paul Feigenbaum recalls, "graduate school gave me both the desire for public engagement and considerable anxiety about whether to pursue it within academia" (n.p.). The problem is not, it seems, a lack of inspiration for community engagement; rather, students need more "systemic means" (Feigenbaum, n.p.) of supporting such engagement, once inspired.

When early-career academics are told that "giving trees don't get tenure" (Perlmutter), and when public engagement is viewed as naive "do-goodism" (Adler-Kassner, Crooks, and Watters 15), graduate programs have little incentive to go public.

On the other hand, graduate-level service-learning has often been lauded as a way of offering *vocational* experiences for graduate students, particularly those in social work, gerontology, nursing, and education. This vocational sentiment is, on occasion, echoed in writing studies—see, for example, Rentz and Mattingly's argument that professional writing graduate students should consider "caring for others" as always secondary to the goal of professionalism and real-world applications of school-derived knowledges and practices.

I do not suggest that graduate programs should exclude either professional development or community wellness from their community outreach agendas (for a compelling example of the latter, see Kimme Hea). However, in reviewing my co-authors' critical reflections, I find that there is something to be gained by thinking about graduate writing studies primarily in terms of *civic responsibility*. Resting somewhere between a logic of expertise and the uncritical charitability that service-learning scholars and teachers have long criticized, civic responsibility is an invitation for graduate students to think about their emerging expert identities in a world fraught with conflicting values and unevenly distributed resources. Not in addition to, but *as a means of* preparing students to be the best writers, thinkers, teachers, and whatever-ers, graduate programs must provide lenses through which students will recognize their work as situated within complex social and political networks (including those we attempted to map on the board during class), to which they are inescapably accountable.

In reviewing these critical reflections, which trace our struggles to adapt our theories and practices in response to negotiated community relationships, I urge graduate programs in writing studies (including my own) to more consciously support graduate students' sense of civic responsibility, broadly defined. This does not mean graduate programs should establish institutionalized service-learning projects or specify volunteer hours as a degree requirement. Rather, programs might begin by carefully evaluating their mission statements (*Are we concerned with our students' roles as citizens and community members?*), their course offerings (*Do we teach students how to engage with publics?*), and their mentorship culture (*Do we habitually provide for students' ambitions for civic engagement?*) in order to recognize and support civic responsibility as a core element of graduate education.

End Notes

1. We recognize that, in these reflections, we focus exclusively on the student experience and do not directly include the voices of community members who partnered with us to run the tutorial sessions. Far from unimportant, those perspectives were a crucial element in our course, the impact of which my co-authors measure in their reflections. Still, we regret that the scope of this essay does not include a better articulation of the community members' individual interests and learning outcomes, nor does it include their assessments of what students did and should gain from their work together. We challenge our readers to follow with a critical analysis of a graduate community literacy course that directly involves community partners in evaluating course outcomes.

2. All community members' names have been replaced by pseudonyms.

Works Cited

Adler-Kassner, Linda, Robert Crooks, and Ann Watters, eds. *Writing the Community: Concepts and Models for Service-Learning in Composition*. Washington, D.C.: American Association of Higher Education/NCTE, 1997.

Banks, Adam. *Race, Rhetoric, and Technology: Searching for Higher Ground*. Mahwah, NJ: Lawrence Erlbaum, 2006.

Bizzell, Patricia. "Composition Studies Saves the World!" *College English* 72.2 (2009): 174-187.

Cushman, Ellen and Jeff Grabill. "Writing Theories/Changing Communities: Introduction." *Reflections on Community-Based Writing Instruction* 7.4 (2009): 1-20.

Cushman, Ellen. "The Rhetorician as an Agent of Social Change." *College Composition and Communication* 47.1 (1996): 7-28.

Day, Jennifer Cheeseman. *Population Projections of the United States by Age, Sex, Race, and Hispanic Origin: 1995 to 2050*. U.S. Bureau of the Census, Current Population Reports, P25-1130. U.S. Government Printing Office, Washington, DC: 1996. Web. 5 Sep. 2014.

Deans, Thomas. "Sustainability Deferred: The Conflicting Logics of Career Advancement and Community." *Unsustainable: Re-imagining Community Literacy, Public Writing, Service-Learning, and the University*. Ed. Jessica Restaino and Laurie JC Cella. Lexington, 2013: 101-111.

Dewey, John. *Democracy and Education*. New York: Macmillan, 1916.

Feigenbaum, Paul. "The Push and Pull of Being Publicly Active in Graduate School." *Reflections* 7.3 (2008). Web. <http://reflectionsjournal.net>

Fero, Michele, Jim Ridolfo, Jill McKay Chrobak, Deborah Vriend Van Duinen, Jason Wirtz, Ellen Cushman, and Jeffrey T. Grabill. "A Reflection on Teaching and Learning in a Community Literacies Graduate Course." *Community Literacy Journal* 1.2 (2008): 81-93. <http://www.communityliteracy.org/index.php/clj>

Fish, Stanley. *Save the World on Your Own Time*. Cambridge: Oxford UP, 2008.

Fleckenstein, Kristi. *Vision, Rhetoric, and Social Action in the Composition Classroom.* Carbondale: Southern Illinois UP, 2009.

Flower, Linda. *Community Literacy and the Rhetoric of Public Engagement.* Carbondale, IL: Southern Illinois UP, 2008.

Freire, Paulo. *Pedagogy of the Oppressed.* 1970. New York, NY: Continuum, 2012.

Gimarc, Ryan. "Migration of Michigan's Young Knowledge Population." *Michigan Economic Workforce Indicators and Insights* (Winter 2014). Bureau of Labor Market Information & Strategic Initiatives. 12. PDF file.

Goldblatt, Eli. *Because We Live Here: Sponsoring Literacy Beyond the College Curriculum.* Cresskill, NJ: Hampton Press, 2007.

Grabill, Jeffrey T. "Community-Based Research and the Importance of a Research Stance." *Writing Studies Research in Practice: Methods and Methodologies.* Ed. Lee Nickoson and Mary P. Sheridan. Carbondale: Southern Illinois UP, 2012. 210-219.

Heller, Caroline E. *Until We Are Strong Together: Women Writers in the Tenderloin.* New York, NY: Teachers College Press, 1997.

Herzberg, Bruce. "Community Service and Critical Teaching." *College Composition and Communication* 54.3. (1994): 307-319.

hooks, bell. *Teaching to Transgress: Education as the Practice of Freedom.* New York: Routledge, 1994.

Howard, Ursula. "History of Writing in the Community." *Handbook of Research on Writing.* Ed. Charles Bazerman. New York: Lawrence Erlbaum, 2008. 237-254.

Joseph, Miranda. *Against the Romance of Community.* Minneapolis: U of Minnesota P, 2002.

Kimme Hea, Amy. "Developing Stakeholder Relationships: What's at Stake?" *Reflections* 4.2 (2005). Web. <http://reflectionsjournal.net>

Long, Elenore. *Community Literacy and the Rhetoric of Local Publics.* West Lafayette: Parlor Press, 2008.

Mathieu, Paula. *Tactics of Hope: The Public Turn in English Composition.* Portsmouth, NH: Heinemann. 2005.

McKee, Heidi, and Kristine Blair. "Older Adults and Community-Based Technological Literacy Programs: Barriers & Benefits to Learning." *Community Literacy Journal* 1.7 (2006): 13-39.

Michigan Department of Technology, Labor, and Budget. *Unemployment Statistics: Annual Jobless Rate, Houghton County, 2011.* Web. 5 Sep. 2014. <http://milmi.org/cgi/ dataanalysis/AreaSelection.asp?tableName=Labforce>

Michigan Technological University Career Services. *Michigan Technological University Annual Placement Report: 2011-2012.* Dec. 2012. <http://www.mtu.edu/career/about/pdfs/ annualreport11-12.pdf>.

Michigan Technological University. *2010-2011 Salary Book.* 8 Feb. 2011. <http://usg.mtu.edu/ usg/documents/other/2010-11%20Salary%20Book.pdf>.

Morton, Keith. "The Irony of Service: Charity, Project and Social Change in Service-Learning." *Michigan Journal of Community Service Learning* 2 (1995): 19-32.

Peck, Wayne Campbell, Linda Flower, and Lorraine Higgins. "Community Literacy." *College Composition and Communication* 46.2 (1995): 199-222.

Perlmutter, David D. "Know the Vital Players in Your Career: You." *Chronicle of Higher Education*. 11 Aug. 2014. Web. 12 Aug. 2014.

Rentz, K., & Mattingly, A. (2006). "Selling Peace in a Time of War: The Rhetorical and Ethical Challenges of a Graduate-Level Service-Learning Course." *Reflections* 4(2), 103–122.

Selber, Stuart. *Multiliteracies for a Digital Age*. Carbondale, IL: Southern Illinois UP, 2004.

Smith, Aaron. "Older Adults and Technology Use." *Pew Research Internet Project*. 3 Apr. 2014. Web. <http://www.pewinternet.org/files/2014/04/PIP_Seniors-and-Tech-Use_040314.pdf>

Stuckey, J. Elspeth. *The Violence of Literacy*. Portsmouth: Heinemann, 1991.

U.S. Census Bureau. American Community Survey 3-Year Estimates, 2010-2012. "Table DP03: Selected Economic Characteristics." *American FactFinder*. 2011. Web. 5 Sep. 2014.

U.S. Census Bureau. Gazetteer Files. "National Counties Gazetteer File." *United States Census 2010*. Washington: U.S. Census Bureau, 22 Aug. 2012. Web. 5 Sep. 2014.

U.S. Census Bureau. Statistical Abstracts. "Table 14: State Population--Rank, Percent Change, and Population Density: 1980 to 2010." *Statistical Abstract of the United States: 2012* (131st ed.). Washington: U.S. Census Bureau, 2011. Web. 5 Sep. 2014.

Author Bios

Lauren Marshall Bowen is an Assistant Professor and Director of Composition in the Humanities Department at Michigan Technological University, which houses Rhetoric, Theory, and Culture (RTC) PhD and MS programs. Her work has appeared in *College Composition and Communication and College English*.

Kirsti Arko is the Assistant Director of the Michigan Tech Multiliteracies Center, in addition to being a PhD student in the RTC program. Her research interest is in writing tutors in the STEM field and their transfer of writing center experience to a STEM professional context.

Joel Scott Beatty is a PhD student in the RTC program at Michigan Technological University. He also teaches Film, Public Speaking and Multimedia Communication in MTU's undergraduate humanities programs.

Cindy Delaney is a MS student in the RTC program at Michigan Technological University where she also teaches Honors Composition for first- and second-year students.

Isidore Kafui Dorpenyo is a PhD student in the RTC program at Michigan Technological University. He teaches an undergraduate course in Professional and Technical communication. He has also taught first-year Composition.

Laura Moeller is a MS student in the RTC program at Michigan Technological University, and a Master's student in American Studies at the University of Dortmund, Germany. At Michigan Tech, she has taught German and first-year composition.

Elsa Roberts is a MS student in the RTC program at Michigan Technological University. She also teaches Composition and Diversity Studies in Michigan Tech's undergraduate humanities program. Her research focus is on women's everyday experience bicycling and the impact of gender on their experience, as well as the importance of community in their cycling choices.

John Velat is the director and principal investigator of the Eastern Tribal Technical Assistance Program (TTAP) and a PhD Student in the RTC program, both at Michigan Technological University. His research interests are in risk and technical communication and he teaches workshops on transportation development, management, and safety for American Indian governments.

Discordant Place-Based Literacies in the Hilton Head, South Carolina Runway Extension Debate

Emily Cooney

In making a case for ecocomposition, Sidney Dobrin has claimed that writing, place, and environment cannot be separated. As Donehower, Hogg, and Schell and Deborah Brandt might argue, literacy cannot be separated from place either. But it might sometimes be separated from environment as an ecosystem that has value distinct from, and without the influence of, humans. In the Hilton Head, South Carolina airport runway extension debate, how stakeholders read, write, and speak of the land next to the airport is inherently connected to how they interact with that place and with each other. But they do not read and write of the land as a valuable ecosystem. Opposition to the runway extension has nothing to do with environmental impacts. The place is valued for economic, social, and historical reasons. As an environment, it is not much considered.

In making a case for ecocomposition, Sidney Dobrin claims that "writing and rhetoric cannot be separated from place, from environment, from nature, or from location" (Dobrin 13). As Donehower, Hogg, and Schell and Deborah Brandt might argue, literacy cannot be separated from place either. But it might sometimes be separated from environment as an ecosystem that has value distinct from, and without the influence of, humans. In the Hilton Head, South Carolina airport runway extension debate, how stakeholders read, write, and speak of the land next to the airport is inherently connected to how they interact with that place and with each other. But they do not read and write of the land as a valuable ecosystem. Opposition to the runway extension has nothing to do with environmental impacts. The place is valued for economic, social, and historical reasons. As an environment, it is not much considered.

Hilton Head Airport Runway Extension: An Overview

The Hilton Head Airport, located on the north end of a small sea island off the coast of South Carolina, announced in 2010 that it will extend a runway in order to allow larger and fuller planes to land on the island. The extension will require the removal of a large area of trees. Currently, it has not been actualized, but the project has received approval of funding from the Federal Aviation Administration (FAA) and state and local governments. And the developers have recently completed an environmental assessment (EA) finding no significant impact. These signs suggest the extension is moving forward.

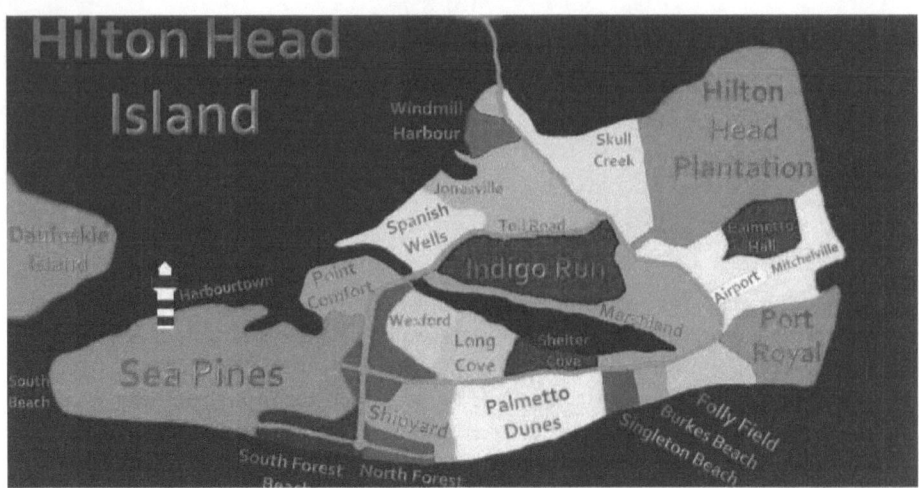

Figure 1: Map of Hilton Head Island

The trees to be cut, and the airport, are located on land that has been used and lived on by the Gullah descendants of freed slaves since the mid-nineteenth century. They founded the town of Mitchelville in the area. On the map, Mitchelville is the area above Port Royal on the far right of the island (see fig. 1). The airport is highlighted within that section. There is also a relatively new residential development and golf course called Palmetto Hall, which, on the map, is the maroon area that carves into Mitchelville. Neither the Mitchelville nor Palmetto Hall residents support the plan to increase the length of Hilton Head airport's runway. Residents of the south end of Hilton Head, which is the more developed end and is located on the left side of the map, support the extension of the runway because it will supposedly allow larger and fuller planes to land on the island. They believe the extension will enable more tourists to visit, which will increase income from golfing and resort vacations.

The residents of Mitchelville, specifically those who are members of the church located directly next to the future runway extension—St. James Baptist Church—have held two rallies in opposition to the proposal, including one on April 11, 2010. The residents of Palmetto Hall, located across the street from the airport, have also vocalized their opposition to the extension and are using the official public meetings to lodge complaints. In support of this proposal, the town of Hilton Head has held many town council meetings including: a Master Plan presentation on October 27, 2010, a meeting for questions before the presentation of the EA on April 3, 2012 and a meeting for questions after the presentation of the EA on June 27, 2012 which determined a "Finding of No Significant Impact."[1] The local newspaper, *The Island Packet*, has been reporting on the events as they have been unfolding. Along with the YouTube videos of the April 11 St. James rally and the published minutes from town council meetings, *The Island Packet* is one of the main public outlets for all stakeholders including Mitchelville and Palmetto Hall residents against development, and south islanders, developers and the local government for development. It is in these published, public interactions and engagements between stakeholders that a hierarchy of place-based literacies is revealed.

The debate unfolding necessarily requires particular literacies of the treescape currently in the path of the future runway extension. That is, it requires particular ways of knowing and reading the place in question. For the developers and supporters of the runway extension and even Palmetto Hall residents, the discourse is built from literacies of development-based economics. The land represents economic value either through being developed or by supporting the value of already existing developments. The supporters see increased income potential because a larger runway means larger planes, which means more tourists. Palmetto Hall residents see the trees as property value assurance both aesthetically and as a buffer for airport noise. This way of understanding the land is place-based, but it is not place-specific. It is a way of seeing any plot of land with trees and it is driven by developers who are not local to Hilton Head, but national and international. James Guignard explains how outside developers bring generic place-based knowledge to specific places in his examination of fracking in Pennsylvania. He argues, "Industry uses a nationalized, displacing rhetoric that abstracts the region…[and] ignores local knowledge in favor of their own language and practices" (Guignard 4). By abstracting the land and trees in question, supporters of the runway *and* Palmetto Hall residents have minimized the environmental, social, and historical values and emphasized the economic.

For the residents of Mitchelville, however, the place is very specific. Their discourse is built from social and historical literacies. While the other stakeholders see the land as (sub)urban, Mitchelville residents see it decidedly as what Donehower, Hogg, and Schell would term *rural*. In their book, the authors define rural literacies as, "The particular kinds of literate skills needed to achieve the goals of sustaining life in rural areas—or…to pursue the opportunities and create the public policies and economic opportunities needed to sustain rural communities" (Donehower, Hogg, and Shell 4). The Mitchelville residents appear in their public discourse to have the first part of this definition as their goal. The aim is to sustain their way of life and their ways of reading, seeing and using that place. They want the land to remain as is because it is part of *their* community. It is undeveloped not because of missed opportunity, but because it is a rural part of a historically rural area. These residents' very particular place-based literacy is at a distinct disconnect with two major factors in the runway debate. First, it clashes with the urban or suburban-based literacies held by the other stakeholders. Second, in the way the Mitchelville residents publicly present the goal of sustaining their way of life, they are not looking to "pursue the opportunities and create the public policies and economic opportunities" needed to sustain that way of life. In fact, as this paper suggests, they are at times actively rejecting certain paths towards those policies. Specifically, they are rejecting environmental literacies. So, too, are all other publicly active stakeholders in the debate. So the Mitchelville residents are missing an opportunity—perhaps, as the rally reveals, purposefully—to take on an additional place-based environmental literacy that could help them achieve their goal of stopping the runway extension. The result of these two disconnects is an almost foregone conclusion that the extension will be developed without anyone ever publicly taking up the cause of environmentalism.

The Role of Discourse and Literacy in the Hilton Head Airport Runway Debate

Sidney Dobrin argues we should be focusing on "understanding how discursive construction interacts with [the places we inhabit], builds those places, maps those places, defines those places, and ultimately controls those places" (Dorbin 24). The discursive constructions of stakeholders in the Hilton Head case are what *should* build a shared place-based literacy. The published, public presentations and reactions from multiple stakeholders reveal two unequal literacies instead. In this paper, I aim to determine how the developers manage to maintain control over the public discourse and why the Mitchelville stakeholders, who use the only dissenting literacy, are willing to let those in control be the only voice on environmental matters.

Deborah Brandt's theories of literacy are a useful starting point. *Literacy as Involvement* shares Brandt's theory of writing and reading as requiring an active participation and acknowledgement between writer and reader that must take the place of corporeal interactions. She explains:

> Readers must be able to see illocutionary presence despite corporeal absence and to see how a text relates to their own presence on the scene, to what they, as readers, are doing moment to moment. Only by maintaining this intimate awareness can readers carry out the work of reading. Authors also trade on this awareness with frequent references, both direct and oblique, to the acts of writing and reading in progress, and with language that indexes the developing history of joint writer-reader accomplishments (*Literacy as Involvement* 87).

The necessity of following along with a written argument is that both reader and writer acknowledge each other and what they both must agree on in order for understanding to occur. In the Hilton Head case, this necessary component is often missing—not only in written discourse, but also in spoken. Stakeholders either do not acknowledge each other in their writing and speaking or they mock each other. This is evident at the St. James rally when a prominent citizen, Dr. Emory Campbell, publicly dismisses an environmental literacy of the contested land by mocking coastal animal and plant conservation efforts. Instead, he promotes social and historical literacies by emphasizing the Mitchelville community's long history of living on that land and their connection to the slaves who settled it. As another example, one letter to the editor by a south island resident, Mr. Faust, explicitly makes fun of a group who wants to save "two trees" rather than dozens of lives. The tree-savers are not publicly active enough to have published any easily findable objections. But more importantly, Mr. Faust shows an outright disdain for environmental concern. Both of these examples will be explored in detail later, but for now it is important to point to their competing literacy practices. Both men mock an opposition that comes from an environmental reading of the land, but they also cannot agree on the correct way to read, write, or speak of the land. There is dissonance.

That dissonance of literacy practices appears to make shared understanding or communication impossible. The developers, south island residents, and newspaper have a public discourse deriving from literacies of development-based economics. Even one opposition group, the Palmetto Hall residents, uses that discourse. The Mitchelville residents reject that discourse entirely and, in turn, the other stakeholders reject Mitchelville's social and historical literacies. Brandt explains, "Literacy is a resource...a means of production and reproduction, including a means by which legacies of human experience move from past to future and by which, for many, identities are made and sustained" (*Literacy in American Lives* 6). Brandt goes on to note that there are "multiple literacy practices" developing differently depending on context and location of learning that are not only a sign of "cultural variety" but "also a sign of stratification and struggle" (8). Position in society is often reflected *and* shaped by literacy practices. Whether a person or group is taken seriously in a public debate can depend heavily on the literacy practices they bring. The literacies that have the most impact on the Hilton Head runway debate reveal an almost foregone conclusion that the extension will happen. They are the literacies of those who are responsible for the project. The discourses taking place in the public sphere most often come from those literacies—those of development-based economics.[2] Other literacies, including other ways of knowing the place and other ways of reading and writing, sometimes make an appearance, but they are not sustained and they do not alter that foregone conclusion. It is as if a stalemate has occurred among stakeholders because they are not fluent in each other's literacies. This appears to be the case for all points but one. Each community stakeholder group has conceded to the developers and government that there will be no real environmental harm from the runway extension. Something about how the developers and FAA presented their findings to the public gave the impression that this was an aspect of the proposal not to be challenged.

Brandt's concept of literacy practices suggests that our ways of being literate become defining parts of who we are as individuals and groups. Literacy takes on a kind of materiality because it is identificatory.[3] Stakeholders understand their particularities through and because of their literacies. In Hilton Head, it makes it difficult not only to understand other stakeholders, but also to grasp the best ways of addressing those other groups. If dominant stakeholders are controlling the public sphere and locked into their discourse because it develops from identity-forming literacy, their ability to share in the meaning-making Brandt writes of in *Literacy as Involvement* is undeveloped. And the Mitchelville residents face the doubly difficult task of manipulating their own discourse to include the dominant literacies *and* represent their own. So far, Mitchelville stakeholders have actively and vocally chosen not to manipulate their discourse. It is obvious those using the dominant discourse feel no need to manipulate their own, either. Instead, they all use their specific place-based literacies to "[function] as a tool to identify...with one cultural group and to dis-identify with another group" (Donehower 49). Across the board there is a lack of recognition, a lack of understanding, and a lack of desire to recognize or understand.

The Difference between Hilton Head and Previous Case Studies

Case studies of similar disputes have been instrumental in distinguishing how and why sites of disagreement arise in order to come to conclusions about how to move forward. But they have predominantly included at least one stakeholder group that represents environmental concern. Studies such as Steven B. Katz and Carolyn R. Miller's "The Low-Level Radioactive Waste Siting Controversy in North Carolina," Hannah Scialdone-Kimberly and David Metzger's "Writing in the Third Space from the Sun," and Peter Goggin and Elenore Long's "The Co-Construction of a Local Public Environmental Discourse" have furthered rhetorical understanding of how environmentalism is perceived and acted out in real-world situations. They each highlight the public encounters that occur when environmental issues are brought forward. But what happens when a real-world situation that will adversely affect a real, physical environment is not publicly and consistently approached from any environmentalist perspective? The Hilton Head case reveals that perhaps what happens is that the assurance from the local government and corporations who want the runway extension that there will be no significant harm is accepted as good enough and stakeholders against development forego a chance to unite and/or stop the construction.

The disconnects between place-based literacies appear to be a major factor in why those in opposition have not joined forces or taken on an environmental literacy. In the Hilton Head airport runway dispute, the rural, place-based literacies of the Mitchelville community are historical and social. For example, at a rally held at St. James church in Mitchelville residents and supporters speak of their connections to the church and the amount of time their families have lived in Mitchelville. But they are not in control of the majority of public discourse. Michelle Simmons' bases her analysis of citizen participation in environmental policy on the premise that "it is the institutions…with their rules and practices that determine the ways in which citizens participate in the production of environmental decisions and policy" (Simmons 10). In the case of the Hilton Head runway, those in power have created a public discourse that emphasizes literacies of development-based economics. Mitchelville's historical and social literacies, and virtually all environmental literacies, rank lower in the hierarchy and are often ignored by those in power and those reporting on the debate. For example, there was no official, public response to the St. James rally by either the local government or the airport developers. And while the newspaper did cover that event, the majority of articles about the runway extension are in terms of development and economics and not in terms of historical, social, or environmental significance of the place. This is especially evident in the articles covering the meeting after the presentation of the environmental assessment in which only Palmetto Hall residents are quoted and concerns are limited to property values and noise increase.

So far, case studies focus on instances in which the public addresses sustainability or environmental concerns. Katz and Miller's study of allowing a radioactive waste site in North Carolina deals with how communication in a hotly disputed situation plays out and its effect on community relationships. Their approach to the waste-siting controversy focuses on "the rule-making process of the Authority and on the specific provisions it developed for involving the public…[and] where assumptions about the nature of communication and the role of the public come to the surface" (Katz and Miller 116). That is, they examine how the general public is perceived by the "Authority" when it raises questions about the environmental and health impacts of allowing a radioactive waste site in their county. They study a situation centered on a pressing and clear environmental concern and find an "intensity of public dissatisfaction" as a result (Katz and Miller 113). While the public Katz and Miller encounter is different from the public in Hilton Head, their study reveals important components of similar stakeholder relationships. They analyze "the ways in which communication structures the relationship between communities" through the interactions the Authority sponsors between itself and the public, including its communication of risk to the residents directly affected by the waste site (Katz and Miller 116). What Katz and Miller find appears to hold true in the Hilton Head case as well:

> Communication takes place between parties who have different…knowledge about the risk and different degrees of access to power; the parties are often characterized as "experts" on the one hand and citizens, laypeople, or the general public on the other. In decision-making contexts, risk communication developed as an attempt to overcome these differences by "correcting" the public's "risk perceptions" so that they would better match the "risk analyses" made by the experts (116).

In the case of the waste-siting controversy, the public continued to express concern, but this method of "correcting" any perception of environmental harm seems to have worked well in Hilton Head. Each "non-expert" group defers the matter of environmental impact to the experts without publicly vocalizing any concerns.

Scialdone-Kimberly and Metzger's case study examines the *multiple* stakeholders who represent their environmental concerns at the 2007 United Nations Forum on Forests. In this study, the authors focus on how stakeholders understand their roles in the forum knowing that "guaranteeing a place in the dialogue [does] not guarantee stakeholders a place from which they [can] be heard" (Scialdone and Metzger 40). Their use of Burke's pentad as a lens for reading the forum allows them to focus on how groups identify themselves with each other and with the Authority, the United Nations, when publicly presenting their arguments on forest sustainability. Scialdone-Kimberly and Metzger's conclusion is that stakeholders can affect sustainable change even when interacting with a powerful group such as the United Nations "when [sustainability's] discursive burdens are also acknowledged and addressed" (51). The keys to the positive takeaway of this case study are a willing Authority in the United

Nations and an acknowledgement of "discursive burdens." In the Hilton Head case, there is neither a willing Authority nor an acknowledgement that there are natural and seemingly unconquerable discursive conflicts between stakeholders. Without the glue of a shared goal, those with authority and those without do not seem to be able to share a discourse either.

Goggin and Long examine the role of the public in promoting sustainable practices. The authors analyze a collection of letters to the editor in a Bermudan newspaper, the *Royal Gazette*, written by citizens concerned over a proposed hotel development along a strip of beachfront property. Goggin and Long expect that the study "can teach us about the limits and possibilities of constructing democratic discourse about the environment that is at once focused and sustained and also accessible to local people" (11). In this instance, the community is utilizing public discourse to create a community literacy about an event that will affect their lives and their environment. Goggin and Long have some unusual fortune and are able to examine letters that have been published in their entirety by the newspaper and argue, "Few information venues have as much outreach and influence in promoting and informing literacies of environment and sustainability in the lives of ordinary people as the daily news media" (6). The unchanged letters to the editor may reveal a coalition between two stakeholders, the residents and the newspaper, because of their shared environmental concern. In this case, groups in the community use environmental discourse to achieve their end goal of halting the development of beachfront property. The local newspaper, by publishing these letters in their entirety, appears to choose sides in the argument, and they have not chosen to align with the developers. Stakeholders in the Hilton Head case can also be seen working together and sharing a discourse. But *The Island Packet*, Hilton Head's daily newspaper, does not actively participate in the alliance the way Bermuda's *Royal Gazette* appears to do. Instead, *The Island Packet* reflects the alliance in the way stories of the runway extension are written. For example, there is a stock reason for the runway extension that seems to accompany most articles in a variation similar to this one written by Tom Barton in October 2010: "The current runway and tree obstructions force airlines to reduce aircraft weight and fly them at less than capacity, making routes less profitable and less likely to continue, [airport officials] said" (Barton). As opposed to the *Royal Gazette*, this newspaper does not seem to be obviously allying with stakeholders who oppose the runway extension, but discretely aligning with those who support it as articles are almost always from the perspective of the "progress" of the extension. And neither the newspaper nor Mitchelville and Palmetto Hall residents publicly speak of the place with any environmental literacy. The newspaper maintains a discourse using the (sub)urban development-based economic literacies of the developers, government sponsors, airlines, and south island residents. The groups who oppose the runway do not even publicly acknowledge each other very often. Perhaps unsurprisingly, their appearances in public debates are not as unified or as prevalent as the developers, airlines, and south island residents.

Shaping the Dominant Discourse through Literacies of Development-based Economics

The presentations held by the town council on the extension Master Plan and the EA reveal a specific literacy of development-based economics that has come to dictate the dominant discourse of the Hilton Head debate. Michele W. Simmons emphasizes in her introduction a focus that "involves investigating the power relations and resulting subject positions that inhibit or encourage significant citizen participation in the decisions of environmental policy" (Simmons 10). She claims current models of environmental risk communication do not work because communicators present findings in one-way models and "do not account for cultural differences across communities" even though "public participation should be determined by real and localized situations, not hypothetical, decontextualized questions" (Simmons 27). Because the Hilton Head runway extension requires tree removal and trimming, the project requires an EA. But the requirement of assessment and the assessment itself have been shaped and determined by those in power. So the discourse of environmentalism in this project has remained stagnant and unchallenged by other stakeholders with different cultural ties to the area and different literacies. Interestingly, there are significant public responses to the developers by the Palmetto Hall residents in these official meetings, especially after the EA is released. But the Mitchelville residents are glaringly absent from both the reports published by the council and the newspaper articles covering the events. As established in the previous section, multiple stakeholders have *access* to the public sphere. However, in these official settings the sphere requires a particular type of discourse in order for a group's argument to be validated. And the presentation of information brings with it the assurance that the project and the tree removal/trimming are going to happen. The Palmetto Hall residents, as opposed to those from Mitchelville, maintain the discourse of economics in their official complaints. So their complaints are heard. They are recorded in the official minutes and newspaper accounts. But even as they are heard, the project continues to move forward.

In the "Hilton Head Airport Master Plan Update" presentation put forth on October 27, 2010, the project team highlights sixteen town meetings/presentations about the project since August 2009. Of those, only three included comments and/or questions from the public. During the presentation, the Master Plan was highlighted the steps that have been made toward achieving the plan and those still needed to be made. Included in the latter is a section dedicated to what they label "Environmental Considerations" that includes, but is not limited to, considerations of air quality, compatible land use, hazardous materials, and socioeconomic impact/environmental justice. None of the items on that list had been performed to as of October 27, 2010. Materiality theorist Ronald Greene argues, "[W]e should focus on how rhetoric distributes different elements on a terrain of a governing apparatus"(38). In this instance, the focus should be on what elements are not being distributed on the terrain. Not only is environmentalism only nodded to by way of explaining how the EA will take place, the conditions of the Mitchelville residents and the trees set to be clear-cut do not warrant the same nod. The dominant discourse does not even make room in this presentation to better understand the position of the Mitchelville stakeholders. It is not in the dominant group's perceived interests so they put it off until later, when they will present their findings in their own discourse, influenced by their own literacies.

Towards the end of the Master Plan presentation, there is a question-and-answer section. A few questions regarding environmental concerns like tree removal and wetland impact are asked. The responses to the questions are almost rote and remain focused on legal requirements and guidelines. For example, in response to "What is the impact of Alternative 2 on trees, as well as the protected wetlands and buffers," the Master Plan explains, "No *additional* tree removal is anticipated at this time and wetlands impacts…will be permitted in accordance with USACE regulations" (emphasis added, "Master Plan" B-25). Altogether, the presentation regarding the Master Plan works to negate the environmental considerations of the proposal by presenting them and then promising to do the analyses needed while still moving forward with the plans. In fact, included in the presentation are letters from different airlines, the airport board, and federal, state, and county governments giving their approval and commitment to move forward with the extension plan *even though they have not done an EA*. In this instance, the developers as dominant stakeholders are certainly making "judgments about the welfare of a population" in their public presentation without actually considering the discourses of part of the population and without being held responsible for the lack of attention paid to the environmental impact (Greene 39).

On April 3, 2012, the county and developers held a meeting to present initial fieldwork findings in preparation for the EA. The official report states:

> [B]etween 5:00 p.m. to 8:00 p.m., at the Hilton Head Island Branch Library… [t]he project team set up displays that included the proposed time line for the EA and a field work results map. Project team representatives were available to answer questions. A table was set up for those who wished to fill out the public comment form at the meeting ("April 3" 1).

There were seventy-two people present at the meeting and a total of thirty comment cards turned in. The published comments from the meeting reveal a strong presence of the dominant discourse of development-based economics, with many complainants taking up property value, quality of life, and noise pollution as key factors against the project. Comments include: "The FAA should step up and provide necessary financial support to protect the peaceful life of surrounding communities," "[P]lease ensure that future noise standards are considered in the impact analysis," "A key issue, that is now more evident, is ground noise created by aircraft…A 75-foot buffer of trees and shrubs will have little impact on noise mitigation" ("April 3" 2-3).

There are a few comments that are not in the dominant discourse, but they are answered in the dominant discourse and they reveal an interesting component of the EA. In answer to, "What about the Church and that beautiful tree?" one of only two comments specifically about St. James church[4] and three about the trees, the officials respond, "The church will remain in its current place…The large trees on church property are to be trimmed as part of the off-airport tree trimming project, which is not part of the environmental assessment being prepared for the extension of the runway" ("April 3" 3). The discourse of the question is cultural and personal. The person asking the question clearly reads and understands that location with a social and/or historical literacy. The discourse of the response is logical and matter-of-fact. Any impediments from the existence of the church and trees have already been overcome and now they are not an issue. The way they seem to have overcome those trees is by keeping them beyond the scope of "airport property." Because the trees are not going to be cut down, they are not subject to an EA. And because the church is out of the path of the runway, any impact is minimal.

The EA itself, while clearly made public, is not easy to find. It is buried on the official city website for Hilton Head within a long list of documents that require a lot of searching to find. The language is dense and the document is ninety-five pages long. And the assessment covers everything initially reported as "needing assessment" in the Master Plan update including "Affected Environment" and "Environmental Consequences" that handle a broad range of issues from land use to historical significance to water and air quality. It is not written in a discourse easily accessible to those with literacy histories that do not include very specific legal, scientific, and economic language. The treatment of the physical space and the trees does not reflect a social or historical way of knowing and reading. But the most important component of the EA is that the final determination is "No Significant Impact." With all of the opposition before and after the presentation of the EA, no one questions this determination in terms of traditional environmental concerns. If those who performed the EA say the wetlands and wildlife will be fine and that appears to be good enough. Opponents vocalize distress over noise and economic impact, but not environmental impact. In this respect those in power have been very successful in mitigating potential problems with moving the project forward. They've maintained tight control.

A clear example of this success is the second meeting held in 2012 to present the findings of the EA. It took place on June 27 during the same time and in the same location as the previous meeting. It is at this meeting that the lack of impactful presence from the Mitchelville stakeholders is most noticeable as the subsequent newspaper article on the meeting quotes only residents of Palmetto Hall and the officially published comments show those same interests of economic impact, noise pollution, and quality of life. Any social or historical literacy of the place and any discourse that reflects those literacies are significantly absent from these two public representations of the meeting held and controlled by those in power. The discourse from the St. James rally is not present. Maintaining the discourse of those in power is the goal of these meetings *and* the EA as a step towards completing the project. Michele Simmons tells us that the Environmental Protection Agency (EPA) "model implies a one-way flow of technical information that positions members of the public as consumers and entities to be managed" (13). In their 1995 article, "Risk Communication, Metacommunication, and Rhetorical Stases in the Aspen-EPA Superfund Controversy," Stratman et al.

reveal further the predetermined nature of communicating EAs and other types of risk assessment:

> The answer seems to be to let people be heard, but in highly formalized, highly controlled ways that will *not interfere* with either EPA's control of protocol or EPA's ownership of risk determination expertise…[I]t is interesting to observe that the guidelines make no mention of ways to handle or acknowledge explicit disagreements over substantive issues; specifically, there is no mention that argumentation and counterargumentation are inevitable during risk controversies, nor is there mention of ways to respond to argumentation as part of the larger communication process. (Emphasis in the original, 13)

For Hilton Head, the one-way communication model seems even more planned than the situations outlined by Simmons and earlier by Stratman et. al. because the presentation is not given by the EPA. Rather, the presentation is given by the project developers in coordination with the local government. So the shaping of communication and discourse remains in the hands of those in power over the project.

The official Master Plan report claims:

> One hundred and twenty-eight people attended the…meeting. Forty-three comment forms were turned in at the meeting, and 64 comment forms were received by mail and email during the 30-day open comment period…Review of the comment forms indicated 66 in favor of the proposed improvements at the Airport and 39 opposed to the improvements (several submitted two comment forms) ("June 27" 1).

Even in this summative language are specific choices to emphasize support and deemphasize opposition. The parenthetical aside that there are not actually 39 people opposed to the project is supposed to be substantial proof that this project is overwhelmingly popular and good. Within the comments, however, we see where those in power have let people be heard. As mentioned earlier, the most prominent opposition comes from Palmetto Hall residents or people who align with the Palmetto Hall residents. And the discourse remains within the limits of economics and development set by those controlling the project: "Mitigate noise for land owners," "Reduction in property values because of noise and tree removal," "Noise barrier needs to be considered" ("June 27" 2). Most of the comments published are in support of the project: "Expect extension of the runway to improve the economy of Hilton Head Island," "The Airport is a vital and important community asset," "Hilton Head Island is a destination location, people need to be able to get to the Island quickly and easily ("June 27" 2)" There is no mention of St. James or Mitchelville specifically. There is no discourse reminiscent of the public discourses that community has used publicly in the past. The presentation and the comments reflect developers' literacies. Even the noise complaints and the one comment about tree removal have to do with property values.

Responding with Dissenting Place-based Literacies

I have been maintaining throughout this paper that the Mitchelville stakeholders are driven by social and historical place-based literacies. Those literacies are the origins of their discourse in this case and they consider the location to be vitally important. The concept of knowing oneself through the surrounding world seems, from their public presence, to be an integral part of the history of Mitchelville. The native islanders of Mitchelville live in a section of Hilton Head that is still largely rural by Donehower, Hogg, and Schell's definition in *Rural Literacies*. In the first chapter of the text, the authors explain rural as "a quantitative measure, involving statistics on population and region as described by the U.S. Census; as a geographic term, denoting particular regions and areas or spaces and places; and as a cultural term, one that involves the interaction of people in groups and communities" (Donehower, Hogg, and Schell 2). While much of the rest of Hilton Head has become a popular destination for golfers and resort vacationers, Mitchelville remains steeped in the cultural traditions of its historic, native residents—the Gullah people descended from slaves. Mitchelville is located on the north end of Hilton Head Island, which is also where the airport is currently located, and is also largely undeveloped compared to the way the south side of the island has been developed. The land has historically been the source of livelihood for Mitchelville residents. This relationship between land and people, so distinctly tied to culture because the land is home to the church and generations of families, means their discourse does not reflect environmental literacies as they are commonly understood. Instead, discussion of the land to be cleared for the runway extension centers on the common notion that their lives, their culture, are literally "rooted" in that land. As such, the dominant stakeholder group, the developers, is not accepting—at least not in publicly available texts—the requests to completely halt progress on the runway extension because it is not being offered in a discourse recognized in the public sphere—which is controlled by the dominant stakeholders.

The original proposal for the runway extension involved purchasing a large parcel of land currently used by Mitchelville residents and tearing down St. James Baptist Church, an institution that has been in that place since the 1860s. This church, being such a part of the history of these stakeholders is, in many ways, what Brandt terms a "literacy sponsor" for its members and community. Brandt explains, "Sponsors... are any agents, local or distant, concrete or abstract, who enable, support, teach, and model, as well as recruit, regulate, suppress or withhold literacy...[they] set the terms for access to literacy and wield powerful incentives for compliance and loyalty" (*Literacy in American Lives* 19). The residents, as is proven in the rallies against the extension, see the church as a vital part of their identities. It is a historical root for them to the place they live. The trees on the property are not the important, knowledge-building part of that history. It is the church that sponsors how the residents see, read, and know that land. Because it is this place that has been chosen for the extension, in the debate the residents of Mitchelville speak of "roots [that] go deep" in the land and in the church ("Gullah/Geechee Nayshun Nyews with Queen Quet YouTube Ep 30 Pt 3").

They do not speak of the environmental impact a runway would have on the land. The discourse they use to reach outside communities is not removed from their particular place-based literacy of the land, the church, and their history. And a compromise with outside environmental discourses—despite both the trees and the people on that land having "roots [that] go deep"—has not yet happened as is evidenced in the April 11, 2010 rally.

On April 11, 2010, the St. James Baptist Church, residents of Mitchelville, and the broader Gullah community held a rally when the church was in danger of being torn down along with the surrounding trees. They met, along with other supporters from Hilton Head, under the trees of St. James' property. Their rally is publicly available on YouTube. It started off, as all Gullah events start off, with an invocation. Throughout the rally, the participants break into call and response hymns as they feel moved to do so. The Reverend begins the invocation with, "[God] let *your* will be done on this island, in this community, in the hearts of your people everywhere…that we might have a reverence for things that are *sacred*, that we might have a reverence, dear God, for your *bethel spots*" (Emphasis added, "YouTube Ep 30 Pt 1"). In this opening prayer, the group has determined it is *their* cause which is sacred, *their* understanding of the land that is God's understanding. And though they understand that this rally is meant to "make some noise," in the public sphere because, as Mr. Young declares, otherwise "nobody will care," the noise they are making is fixed on their own idea of the situation ("YouTube Ep 30 Pt 1"). This immediately closes off their discourse from those in the dominant group and it certainly does not translate into a discourse that the public sphere will readily accept as valid. In this rally, the speakers are literally preaching to the choir.

More telling of the social and historical place-based literacies of the Mitchelville stakeholders than the religious overtones is the public relationship this group has with environmental causes. In his rally speech, Emory Campbell, a well-respected member of the Gullah community and a member of the Gullah/Geechee Cultural Heritage Corridor Commission, attempts to utilize the dominant discourse to point out the disservice constantly being done to the Gullah culture. In his speech he also makes an adversary of environmentalism and sustainability:

> Over the past forty years we have witnessed consistent displacement of one of… America's most unique cultures—the Gullah/Geechee culture. These culturalassets have been displaced along the coast because of taxes, waterfront access closures, prohibitive ordinances for use of land, and now we're hearing that we need a longer runway for the airplanes. We have watched the town and county over the years protect the trees, wildlife, wetlands, special programs for turtles [laughter], and even alligators [more laughter]. And I believe it's time now for them to recognize the value of the indigenous people ("YouTube Ep 30 Pt 2").

Here Dr. Campbell displays an obvious grasp of the dominant discourse. However, in trying to subvert the discourse, and in making environmentalism a foe, his public representation of the Mitchelville and Gullah stakeholder group further removes that group from the dominant discourse in the public sphere. It's an abdication of Mitchelville's place in the debate by intentionally not grounding the discourse of the rally in a literacy to which the dominant stakeholders legally *have* to pay attention. And it is a choice. Clearly, they are familiar with the successes of environmental causes or Dr. Campbell would not have mentioned them and the audience would not have laughed. Brandt notes the lasting influence of context in literacy development. But Donehower, Hogg, and Schell perhaps explain this particular choice most accurately. They write of "the global movement toward increased privatization of public services and toward a market economy...[that] has been promoted as a historical inevitability... [and has] meant the systematic dislocation of people" (Donehower, Hogg, and Schell 10). The sense of inevitability that the runway extension will happen reflects the authors' critique. The Mitchelville stakeholders maintaining their particular literacies even in public discourse is therefore an important and, I want to stress, valid choice. However, the speech reveals the important role environmental causes can play in fighting against development. So Dr. Campbell's opportunity to utilize a place-based literacy that has a proven track record within dominant discourses of other cases is *outweighed* by the immediacy of shared literacies and therefore a shared discourse with the other rally members. Whether the choice not to engage with any dominant literacy is a form of power in itself because development is inevitable or whether the choice is because they just don't want to, what matters is that they are rejecting it in favor of their own social and historical literacies.

The April 11 rally was not only attended by Mitchelville residents and Gullah community members, there were also two residents of the south end of the island in attendance who oppose the runway extension. The speeches made by these men are the closest any speaker at the rally comes to harmonizing environmentalism with the dominant discourse, of which they are members. There are two things of note in recognizing the environmental appeal of these speakers. First, it is the outsiders of the Mitchelville stakeholder group who call for environmentalism, not members of the group. Second, the speeches are inflammatory and accusatory, allowing those of the dominant discourse who want the extension to cast off these appeals as mere "tree-hugging" rhetoric and not as valid concerns about the future of the land. The first council member to speak recalls a comment he made at a recent council meeting, "Well why don't we put this down in Sea Pines [on the south side of the island]? We don't need a golf course down there...We can use the 18th fairway as a nice flight path...Let's hear what the crying would be then" ("YouTube Ep 30 Pt 3") The obvious point the councilman is making, that this extension is being pushed through because it is not proposing to take over valuable south island property, is validating for the group at the rally. However, in the development-based dominant discourse, it can easily be dismissed. After all, putting the runway on a current, profitable golf course would take income away from Hilton Head and the driving factor for the extension is to bring more income to the island. The second speaker, a small plane pilot, is the only speaker at the rally to make connections between clear-cutting the trees and environmental distress. While the first speaker is driven by pathos, the second speaker maintains a tone of logic that reflects the type of discourse most likely to be validated in the public sphere that has been created for this debate. He explains, "As certified by the Federal Aviation Administration and the local airport authority, the Hilton Head airport is safe now without the need to extend the runway one inch" ("YouTube Ep 30 Pt 3") He goes on to say the airport is "safe now without the need to clear-cut thousands of trees on and off airport property...before the runway is extended one inch, or before one tree is unnecessarily removed, the FAA must conduct and authoritative assessment of potential hazards and that has not been done" ("YouTube Ep 30 Pt 3"). This speaker understands the potential in requiring an EA that as of April 11, 2010 had not been done. However, he is not a member of the Mitchelville stakeholder group. His discourse is different from theirs, and his is influenced by a literacy of environmentalism that informs his argument against the extension. This is in direct contrast to the mocking acknowledgement of environmental discourse from Dr. Campbell. The members of the rally, while listening and nodding, do not take up this discourse into their own at later rallies or appeals. And once the environmental assessment was completed and presented, there are no easily findable public proclamations on behalf of environmental concern.

While Dr. Campbell works to distance this stakeholder group from environmental and sustainability rhetorics, and the two south island representatives work to bring the dominant discourse to the rally, another rally speaker, Ethel Rivers, works to make clear the connection between the culture and the land. She says:

> My name is Ethel Green Rivers...I was born on Mitchelville Plantation. October 16, 1918. I joined this church [St. James Baptist] in 1932. I'm a mother of seventeen children [applause]...And I just want to let y'all know, I have root go deep [sic] in the ground...So when you talk about moving St. James you might as well take a dagger and put in right in my heart (YouTube Ep 30 Pt 3).

Rivers' speech uses a place-based literacy that assumes the culture and the land are the same. And it successfully rallies those in attendance. But however moving her story is, it is not relevant to the dominant discourse. This speech is publicly represented as being reflective of the discourse of many Mitchelville residents in attendance. It is in this speech that a major point of discord between the literacies of the Mitchelville stakeholders and those of the dominant group is most clear. The figurative "roots" of Rivers are working as material boundaries surrounding her discourse and thus the public discourse of those she represents in the speech. The church, as she explains, is her literacy sponsor. It shapes how she understands herself and the place where she lives and it shapes how she talks about them as well. In the rally, outside stakeholders attempt to bring in the place-based literacies of the dominant stakeholders and environmentalism to the Mitchelville group, but it is the literacies of Ethel Rivers and Dr. Campbell that they continue to use.

Reporting Events in the Dominant Discourse

The Hilton Head newspaper has reported its observations over the entire course of the debate. *The Island Packet*, begun in 1970, is published by the McClatchy Company and is available in print and online. It serves Hilton Head and its surrounding area. In order for any stakeholder group's message to reach the larger Hilton Head audience the local newspaper must report their stories. Not only that, *The Island Packet* must also allow room for previously unrepresented stakeholders to include their discourse in the dispute by way of letters to the editor. What becomes clear after reading the articles and letters is that the dominant discourse has, on the whole, been adopted by the newspaper and the residents of the south end of the island. There are some citizens who do not approve of the runway extension, but there is still a lack of concern for the environmental impact or sustainable practices. In fact, there is some hostility towards environmentalism even as there is not an obvious group representing the interests of the land. It seems as though in the public sphere of this Hilton Head debate, there is not room for environmental discourse in this particular representative medium, at least not in the articles and letters easily accessed online.

Focusing on articles and letters to the editor in the months of the public presentations I have previously analyzed, the rigid materiality of the dominant discourse and the inability for outside literacies to permeate it in any meaningful way should be clear. In the articles published by *The Island Packet* staff, there are reports on the progress of town council meetings, the progress of the runway extension, the EA presentation, and even reports on the rallies and legal appeals of the Mitchelville stakeholders. But the reports always assume the inevitability of the extension. In an article published about the April 10 rally, the author briefly describes the reasons for the rally, and then goes into a long description of all the government officials who attended:

> Town Councilman Bill Ferguson, who represents Ward 1, where the church is located, urged protesters to "go to the polls and vote accordingly," against the runway expansion...Hilton Head Island mayoral candidates Tom Crews and John Safay, a veteran town councilman, attended the rally. Beaufort County Council member Steve Baer was also in attendance. The airport lies in Baer's district. Safay has said he favors lengthening the runway within the existing boundaries of the airport to allow for future commercial service, if it can be done without harming nearby neighborhoods. Crews said he attended the event largely to listen. "We're having these very strong opinions about the airport with very limited information," he said (Foss).

The article barely mentions members of St. James Baptist Church or Mitchelville residents, but details which officials attended and their opinions on the extension and the rally's message. Mayoral candidate Tom Crews seems even dismissive in his analysis of the event claiming that the "strong opinions" aren't well informed. Of course, there is mention of the rally's discourse: "Members of St. James, which lies under the flight path of planes landing and taking off from the airport, say the runway expansion threatens the native island church, the Gullah-Geechee culture and the future of area residents and businesses" (Foss). The reference to hurting the future of area businesses is mostly in passing, and not at all a focus of the rally.

The article published on October 10, 2010, two weeks before the Master Plan presentation, is similarly lacking in environmental issues, and even lacks statements from anyone in the Mitchelville stakeholder group. There are official government representatives of that group, the same councilmen in attendance at the rally, who speak on behalf of Mitchelville residents, but the residents themselves are missing from the article. In addition, a brief explanation of the "reason" an extension is necessary appears early on in the article. This same explanation appears in many of the articles about the extension, and it seems to come directly from some sort of official statement made by the dominant stakeholders: "The current runway and tree obstructions force airlines to reduce aircraft weight and fly them at less than capacity, making routes less profitable and less likely to continue, [airport officials] said" (Barton). There is no mention of any stakeholders other than the airlines/airport and the customers of those airlines in this oft repeated explanation. The article does mention one community member who opposes the extension and instead focuses on the loss of revenue from Delta airline's choice to stop service to the island. *The Island Packet*, at least in the published articles in the months of April and October 2010, does not seem to represent discourses other than the dominant in any serious way. Thus the discourse put forth at the rally, even though the speakers maintained their literacies, is ineffective in manipulating the dominant discourse represented in the newspaper. And the discourse of environmentalism is still absent from the public discussion of the runway extension case. There is still no room in the dispute, driven heavily by the government/business discourse, for the influence of environmentalism and/or sustainability.

Perhaps the most telling examples of how the dominant discourse traverses multiple stakeholder groups come from the letters to the editor. Most letters come from residents of the south side of the island, which is neither near the airport nor heavily influenced by the rural north end. Like the articles, we see in the letters the maintained dominance of the developers' discourse. Even further, many of the letters express open hostility towards not only the Mitchelville residents, but also environmentalism even though it is largely absent from the public debate.

One example of a letter to the editor that reflects all of the above comes from a south island resident on October 30, 2010. This resident, Bob Faust, has multiple letters published by the newspaper, always in support of the extension and almost always hostile. The author writes, "I thought it was decided to trim the trees to avoid a serious accident and loss of life. Now a group wants to save two trees in exchange for possibly losing 30 to 40 lives. That does not compute on my computer" (Faust). Faust goes on to explain, "The church however is a sensitive, emotional issue. I suggest moving the church to preserve its historical value, or have the town buy it and rebuild it. Whatever is best for the congregation." The author makes two comments that devalue the opinions of stakeholders outside the dominant group. First, his comment on a group that "wants to save two trees" is openly hostile. No airplane accidents have ever occurred at the Hilton Head airport and whatever this group is, they have not been able to vocalize their discourse in public via the rally, the presentations, or the newspaper, so their threat to the extension seems minimal. The second comment, that the church should be moved or purchased by the town to be rebuilt, shows an obvious lack of understanding of the importance of that church in that location to the Mitchelville community and a clear determination to *not* understand the place through their specific social or historical literacies.

The Mitchelville community's concerns are also unmistakably absent from the article covering the EA presentation. Grant Martin writes, "Residents offer comments, critiques of Hilton Head airport environmental assessment," that there was a "largely constructive—but at times contentious—informal meeting" on June 27, 2012. Intriguingly, although the official report states that feedback was overwhelmingly supportive, Martin reports, "Almost all of the input was negative." And while the author states early on that there were concerns about "deforestation" along with noise pollution and property values, there is no other reference to the term in the article. The major focus is on the latter two concerns. Martin quotes several Palmetto Hall residents in response to the claims that the decibel level would not exceed regulatory limits and property values would not be affected: "That explanation was not enough to placate Joe Bradley…'It's been real loud; they must have broken a lot of chainsaws cutting down all those trees already" and, "Another Palmetto Hall resident, Bob DiJianne, said the economic projections fail to take into account a decline in home values…The day they cut these trees,' he said, pointing at a map, 'about 40 to 50 homes are going to lose $100,000 in property value overnight.'" Martin does not quote a Mitchelville resident and ends the report with, "The FAA—which would pay for most of the improvements with money from user fees and taxes on items such as airline fares, air freight and aviation fuel—approved the plan last fall." The entire article, even though it claims residents are concerned about deforestation, maintains the same discourse of economics that the developers have shaped the debate with and that south island residents and Palmetto Hall residents have taken up. At this point, Mitchelville, in the public texts about the debate, is not considered. Its residents' literacies and discourses are not present.

Kim Donehower's discussion of the stigma of rural literacies in the minds of urban and suburban populations bears repeating at this point. She writes, "Literacy function[s] as a tool to identify oneself with one cultural group and to dis-identify with another group that [is] perceived as being of lower status intellectually, culturally, economically, and morally" (Donehower 49). For Donehower, Hogg, and Schell, literacy means "the skills and practices needed to gain knowledge, evaluate and interpret that knowledge, and apply knowledge to accomplish particular goals (4). In the Hilton Head case, the published texts of the dominant group and those that appear to have taken up their discourse (the newspaper, the south island residents, and the Palmetto Hall residents) reveals at least a non-acknowledgement of the Mitchelville discourse and at worst an active disregard in the vein of Donehower's explanation of the urban opinion of rural literacy. The letter written by Bob Faust appears to ignore the rural discourse of the Mitchelville residents *and* actively discredit a relatively un-public environmental argument. The article about the EA presentation does not even offer a disdainful or ignorant representation of the residents. They've been written out of the public debate and any environmental concerns have been successfully excluded.

Conclusion

Bob Faust's letter to *The Island Packet* and Dr. Emory Campbell's speech are examples of how seemingly impermeable place-based literacies can be. Faust's letter, along with the newspaper reports on public presentations and the presentations themselves, reveal the power of development-based economics as place-based literacies. These stakeholders have shaped the dominant discourse which has in turn shaped the Hilton Head debate by requiring their (sub)urban literacies in order to be acknowledged in public discussions. Dr. Campbell's speech, along with Ethel Rivers', reveal the Mitchelville community's clear understanding of the literacy needed to join the debate and their purposeful choice to use their own, rural, place-based literacies instead. Because all stakeholders have locked into their own literacies, the EA performed by the developers has gone unchallenged. Those in support of the project have no need to question the findings. The Palmetto Hall residents, because they are using the developers' literacies, raise only economic concerns. That leaves one major stakeholder group, the Mitchelville community, with an opportunity. But so far, they are missing it. Questioning the findings of the EA would ensure the Mitchelville residents join the dominant discourse because the EA is a legally required step in the development process. Their choice to instead use their social and historical literacies as a challenge to the dominant literacies has meant the project continues to move forward and Mitchelville has been subsumed in the debate. This Hilton Head debate reveals that context is crucial in environmental case studies. Local, place-based literacies play a key role in how national place-based literacies are approached and challenged. Previous case studies like Goggin and Long's about Bermuda and Katz and Miller's about North Carolina reveal groups already using local, place-based environmental literacies. That is not how the Mitchelville residents, or most residents of Hilton Head, see the place to be developed. As a result, the extension will likely happen without ever truly being challenged.

Endnotes

1. The EA claimed to explore all "reasonable" alternatives, that their assessment did not include the tree trimming that would take place "off airport," that they examined everything from soil erosion to noise pollution, and that the FAA determined no significant impact.

2. The public sphere in Hilton Head most accurately reflects Habermas's original conception of the term. While many important scholars have complicated the exclusionary and bourgeois public sphere first described by Habermas, including Michael Warner with

counterpublics and Nancy Fraser's multiplicity of publics, it is this original public sphere theory that shows itself. Habermas' theory is integral to understanding the debate in Hilton Head precisely because it is exclusionary and bourgeois.

3. Ronald Walter Greene explains rhetorical practices as material because of how they occupy institutional structures. Thus, those who are fluent in the right practices get to shape the discourse into what they want and lock others out. Literacies seem to work in the same way in Hilton Head. Which literacy a stakeholder uses affects the success in public discourse.

4. The runway extension plans eventually changed to no longer go through St. James Baptist Church. The church's status as an historical landmark required the developers to realign the runway so that it would pass next to the church, still clear cutting trees in the process. The church would later hold a rally against the new plan as well, due to the noise pollution.

Works Cited

Barton, Tom. "Runway Extension Work Could Begin in 2013." *The Island Packet* [Hilton Head, South Carolina] 19 Nov. 2010. Web. 18 April 2013.

Brandt, Deborah. *Literacy as Involvement: The Acts of Writers, Readers, and Texts.* Carbondale: Southern Illinois UP, 1990. Print.

———. *Literacy in American Lives.* New York: Cambridge UP, 2001. Print.

Dobrin, Sidney I. "Writing Takes Place." *Ecocomposition: Theoretical and Pedagogical Approaches.* Ed. Christian R. Weisser and Sidney I. Dobrin. Albany: State U of New York P, 2001. 11-25. Print.

Donehower, Kim. "Rhetorics and Realities: The History and Effects of Stereotypes about Rural Literacies." *Rural Literacies* Ed. Kim Donehower, Charlotte Hogg, and Eileen E. Schell. Carbondale: Southern Illinois UP, 2007. 37-76. Print.

Donehower, Kim, Charlotte Hogg, and Eileen E. Schell. "Constructing Rural Literacies: Moving Beyond the Rhetorics of Lack, Lag, and the Rosy Past." *Rural Literacies.* Ed. Kim Donehower, Charlotte Hogg, and Eileen E. Schell. Carbondale: Southern Illinois UP, 2007. 1-36. Print.

Faust, Bob. "Don't Sacrifice Interests of Many for Vocal Few." *The Island Packet* [Hilton Head, SC] 30 October 2010: Letter to the Editor. Web. 18 April 2013.

Foss, Cassie. "Protestors on Hilton Head Rally Against Runway Lengthening, Tree Trimming." *The Island Packet* [Hilton Head, SC] 11 Apr. 2010. Web. 18 April 2013.

Fraser, Nancy. "Rethinking the Public Sphere: A Contribution to the Critique of Actually Existing Democracy." *Habermas and the Public Sphere.* Ed. Craig Calhoun. Cambridge: MIT P, 1992. 109-142. Print.

Goggin, Peter and Elenore Long. "The Co-Construction of a Local Public Environmental Discourse: Letters to the Editor, Bermuda's *Royal Gazette*, and the Southlands Hotel Development Controversy." *Community Literacy Journal.* 4.1 (2009): 5-30. Web. 18 April 2013.

Greene, Ronald Walter. "Another Materialist Rhetoric." *Critical Studies in Mass Communication.* 15.1 (1998): 21-40. Web. 18 April 2013.

Guignard, James. "A Certain Uncertainty: Drilling Into the Rhetoric of Marcellus Shale Natural Gas Development." *Environmental Rhetoric and Ecologies of Place.* Ed. Peter N. Goggin. Routledge, forthcoming. 2-22. Print.

Gullah Geechee Nation. "Gullah/Geechee Nayshun Nyews with Queen Quet Ep 30 Pt 1." Online video clip. *YouTube.* YouTube, 12 Apr. 2010. Web. 18 Apr. 2013.

———. "Gullah/Geechee Nayshun Nyews with Queen Quet Ep 30 Pt 2." Online video clip. *YouTube.* YouTube, 12 Apr. 2010. Web. 18 Apr. 2013.

———. "Gullah/Geechee Nayshun Nyews with Queen Quet Ep 30 Pt 3." Online video clip. *YouTube.* YouTube, 12 Apr. 2010. Web. 18 Apr. 2013.

Habermas, Jurgen. *The Structural Transformation of the Public Sphere: An Inquiry into a Category of Bourgeois Society.* Trans: Thomas Burger. Cambridge: MIT P, 1989.

Katz, Stephen B. and Carolyn R. Miller. "The Low-Level Radioactive Waste Siting Controversy in North Carolina: Toward a Rhetorical Model of Risk Communication." *Green Culture: Environmental Rhetoric in Contemporary America.* Ed. Carl G. Herndl and Stuart C. Brown. Madison: U of Wisconsin P, 1996. 111-140. Print.

Martin, Grant. "Residents Offer Comments, Critiques of Hilton Head Airport Environmental Assessment." *The Island Packet* [Hilton Head, SC] 27 Jun. 2012. Web.

Morgan, Cheryl. "Hilton Head Island." Map. *Homes on HHI.* Hilton Head Island Realty and Rentals. 2008. Web. 18 Apr. 2013.

Scialdone-Kimberly, Hannah and David Metzger. "Writing in the Third Space from the Sun: A Pentadic Analysis of Discussion Papers Written for the Seventh Session of the UN Forum on Forests (April 16-27, 2007)." *Rhetorics, Literacies, and Narratives of Sustainability.* Ed. Peter N. Goggin. New York: Routledge, 2009. 39-54.

Simmons, Michele W. *Participation and Power: Civic Discourse in Environmental Policy Decisions.* Albany: State U of New York P, 2008.

Stratman, James F., et al. "Risk Communication, Metacommunication, and Rhetorical Stases in the Aspen-EPA Superfund Controversy." *Journal of Business and Technical Communication.* 9.5 (1995): 5-41. Web. 18 April 2013.

Talbert & Bright. "April 3, 2012 Public Information Meeting." Hilton Head Branch Library. Hilton Head, SC. 3 Apr. 2012.

———. "Hilton Head Airport Master Plan Update." Hilton Head Branch Library. 27 Oct. 2010.

———. "June 27, 2012 Public Information Meeting." Hilton Head Branch Library. 27 Jun. 2012.

Warner, Michael. *Publics and Counterpublics.* New York: Zone Books, 2002. Print.

Wilbur Smith Associates. "Environmental Assessment for the Removal of Tree Obstructions at Hilton Head Airport." "Hilton Head Island Airport/HXD." *Beaufort County*. n.d. Web. 18 April 2013.

Author Bio

Emily Cooney is a fifth year PhD candidate in the Rhetoric/Composition/Linguistics program at Arizona State University. Her main area of study is in the rhetorics of globalization and environmental sustainability. She is also interested in rural and place-based literacies as they relate to issues of globalization and sustainability.

Civic Disobedience: Anti-SB 1070 Graffiti, Marginalized Voices, and Citizenship in a Politically Privatized Public Sphere

Veronica Oliver

>With neither national nor local-level discussions of Senate Bill 1070 adequately addressing bottom line issues such as marginalization, access, and civic engagement, an exploration of marginalized rhetorical acts can provide an informative lens for understanding challenges among marginalized people, their rhetorical tools, and their relations to public spheres. Through an exploration of anti-Senate Bill 1070 graffiti, this article examines how the practice of graffiti points to difference manifesting and playing out in the wider public sphere. It calls for scholars and activists to recognize graffiti as a rhetorical tool worthy of study and cross-cultural discourse.

The "Support Our Law Enforcement and Safe Neighborhoods Act," also known as Senate Bill 1070 (SB 1070), was signed into law by Arizona Governor Janice Brewer on April 23, 2010. This state-specific bill targeting illegal immigration was a response to "solve a crisis…the federal government has refused to fix" (Brewer). While the bill was initially presented as attending to the rising issue of Mexican drug cartels and "border-related violence and crime due to illegal immigration" (Brewer), it should be noted that activity on the Arizona border as a high-level safety threat has been questioned and subsequently contradicted by both Arizona border-town police officials and FBI crime reports (Wagner). Immigration bill SB 1070 has been widely criticized for specifically targeting the Hispanic population in Arizona, including the Department of Justice's concern with probable violations of civil rights, such as the Fourth and Fifteenth Amendment ("Arizona's Immigration"). Examples of these issues include "how 'reasonable suspicion of immigrant status' will be interpreted; and the narrow list of documents eligible to demonstrate lawful presence" (par. 6). While this judicial interruption of the bill signals how democratic ideals can assist in monitoring the level of power states and institutions have in accordance with civil rights, many continue to argue that this legislation unnecessarily criminalizes immigrants, supports racial profiling, and disregards more fine-tuned issues concerning families with mixed U.S. citizen status (Sexton et al.).

In response to criticism of the bill, Governor Brewer has stated that SB 1070 went through "vigorous debate," where she "listened patiently to both sides" (Brewer), yet these statements reflect exclusive discourse among representatives on the issue, such as politicians, lawmakers, and civil rights groups. Equal civic engagement, where the voices of everyday people (non-officials) are heard and reasonably considered, is seldom practiced in public policy decisions despite the wide-reaching effects on the very citizens who are impacted by them. With this in mind, one inherent question is how a targeted marginalized group can enter its voice in a debate that already situates it as having no citizenship status and, subsequently, rights to civic engagement. Since the passing of SB 1070, many grassroots organizations have campaigned against the bill through a variety of counterpublic forms of protest such as a "peaceful non-cooperation" gathering outside the Phoenix, Arizona courthouse ("'Stop SB1070'"), and vigils held outside of detention centers where immigrants await deportation trials as they face the "abuses and inhumane conditions" within ("ACLU"). Of course, such counterpublic tactics and the media coverage that follows garner visibility to these voices that are otherwise often not circulated and heard. That said, for purposes here I turn to one form of publically visible protest that received little attention. In 2010, anti-SB 1070 graffiti found in downtown Phoenix was given brief comment in the news, yet I argue for such political graffiti to be given more importance as a recognized form of civic engagement. In this article, I consider the contemporary significance of graffiti as a rhetorical tool that is carried out by the marking of physical spaces as forums for public dialogue. The importance of taking up this larger question through a discussion of anti-SB 1070 graffiti is that neither marginalized bodies nor their attendant rhetorical tools are often sanctioned equally in the public sphere (Cintron; Fraser; Moreau and Alderman; Young).

Although scholars such as Iris Marion Young and Nancy Fraser discuss broader theories of marginalization in relation to civic engagement, broad-based theories often do not focus on the controversial nature of specific rhetorical tools such as graffiti. As Elenore Long states, it is the local-level practices of civic engagement that offer a "model of local public discourse, one that fills the gap between descriptive accounts of situated literacy and more abstract theories of public discourse" (10). To be clear, larger theoretical discussions of marginalized voices miss the nuances of rhetorical practices working in the everyday to include the exigency of local political issues such as SB-1070 that have wide-reaching implications, as revealed in the prompting of other states creating their own anti-immigration bills following Arizona's move with SB 1070 (Wessler). With neither national nor local-level discussions of SB 1070 adequately addressing bottom line issues such as race, access, marginalization, and civic engagement—which the passing of the bill and subsequent protest responses point to—an exploration of marginalized rhetorical acts, such as graffiti as civic engagement, can provide an informative lens for understanding challenges among marginalized people, their rhetorical tools, and the public spheres in which they work from and in relation to.

The remainder of this essay works in four major parts. First I offer a historical trajectory of graffiti for the purposes of locating it as a rhetorical tradition. While I do not attend to all forms of graffiti or all historical practices, some background provides a way to contextualize an argument for graffiti as an otherwise ignored rhetorical tradition. After establishing graffiti as a rhetorical tradition in its own right, I will discuss the significance of anti-SB 1070 graffiti in order to theorize marginalized bodies, rhetorics, and citizenship. Here, I explicate the power of graffiti to connect physical public spaces and the interrelationship of marginalized bodies and rhetoric in what Jürgen Habermas terms the "larger public sphere"—that discursive arena where citizens come together to hold state power in check. I will bring my discussion into what graffiti can tell us about the current status of citizenship, and thus citizen engagement and the marginalized. In short, political graffiti such as that connected to Senate Bill 1070 offers a rich point of analysis concerning the ways that citizenship as a politics of difference is engaged in the everyday.

While the practice of political graffiti points to how difference manifests and plays out in the dominant public sphere, the final analysis for this project concerns how such work offers a space for what Krista Radcliffe calls *rhetorical listening*. As Ratcliffe explains, rhetorical listening is "a trope for interpretive invention [which] signifies a stance of openness that a person may choose to assume in cross-cultural exchanges" (1). To arrive at such a stance, stakeholders need to recognize how whiteness functions invisibly at different levels in the public sphere; cross-cultural discourse necessitates that we recognize and listen to identifications that share commonalities and differences, opening a space for engagement (32). Ratcliffe argues that "with such borderlands, rhetorical listening helps listeners analyze discursive convergences and divergences" which "helps listeners articulate...identifications and communicate about—and across— both differences and commonalities" (33). Through a consideration of rhetorical listening in relation to normative assumptions of public spaces and rhetorical acts, the final point of argument will explain the importance of recognizing graffiti as a rhetorical tool which can offer a space for rhetorical listening, as these gestures disrupt whiteness from functioning invisibly in the larger public (Ratcliffe 4) by pointing to the absence, and even sometimes criminalization, of marginalized discourses in even the most public of spaces.

Graffiti as a Rhetorical Tradition

Ancient Graffiti

Graffiti has a history dating back to the ancient world, where it could be found "in amphitheatres where crowds gathered and in remote spots where they did not, on walls of buildings, on columns of stoas, on objects" (Baird and Taylor "Preface" xv). Although contemporary graffiti is usually understood as a public act, ancient graffiti was also created in less public spaces, such as "many homes, including [the] wealthy" (Benefiel 20). While the collection of essays in *Ancient Graffiti in Context* vary in how they define graffiti and the groups of graffitists and locations on which they focus, one element of graffiti—that of writing to an audience—is universal. With this in mind, although graffiti's historical relationship to class is more contested than one might assume, one similarity between ancient and contemporary graffiti is how such work reveals that physical public spaces are inherently sanctioned for dominant discourses only.

J. A. Baird's exploration of graffiti found in Dura-Europos at a time when the city was occupied by the Roman military reveals how these personnel marked public spaces where they were stationed with their "name and title" (57-58). Although not examining the possible ideological implications of these military markings, Baird does note how such acts reflect "tak[ing] possession of particular spaces" (56), perhaps revealing "restriction[s] on who might be able to make their mark in such spaces" (59). This question of physical spaces and sanctioned discourse has been approached by other archaeologists and historians who have affirmed the use of ancient graffiti as a subversive tactic by "groups who are otherwise marginalized", such as Pedro Paulo A. Funari who explains that "certain types of pictorial graffiti in Pompeii express aspects of popular culture through caricature thereby critiquing existing power structures and replacing them with alternate narratives" (Baird and Taylor, "Introduction" 11-12). Additionally, Alexei V. Zadorojnyi's discussion of ancient literary figures' attention to graffiti, such as Lucian (AD 125 – after AD 180), reveal the transgressive nature of such acts. In Lucian's *Mimes of the Courtesans*, for instance, two female characters, Chelidonion and Drosis, "realise [sic] that their graffito need to infiltrate the public space in clandestine ways, at night. Chelidonion's graffito will be an act of private, very infrapolitical disobedience but it is still a breach of societal authority" (Zadorojnyi 113). Here, Zadorojnyi's reading of Lucian connects physical public spaces to dominant ideologies, where marginalized others, in this particular case women, do not belong.

Contemporary Graffiti

If ancient graffiti suggests that physical public spaces are inherently marked by dominant political ideologies and that those who are not sanctioned to mark such spaces are transgressing norms, then shifting attitudes and reactions to contemporary graffiti further link such transgressions with marginalized bodies and their attendant rhetorical tools.

One of the earliest public artifacts discussing graffiti is the 1971 *New York Times* article, "'Taki 183' Spawns Pen Pals," where one greek [sic] teenager with the tag name "TAKI 183" became the focus of an editorial covering a then growing trend of tagging one's name and street number on subway trains and throughout the city ("'Taki'"). When the article was written graffiti was "a violation…barred only by Transit Authority rules, not by law" ("'Taki'"). Here it is suggested that graffiti (at least tagging) was, at this point, regarded as an act of youthful indiscretion as opposed to civil disobedience with "…teen-agers from all parts of the city, all races and religions and all economic classes" caught in the act ("'Taki'"). Although this *New York Times* article first places graffiti as an act that is not raced, classed, nor gendered, both the use and association of graffiti would soon become a discourse marker for marginalized others, subsequently leading to its criminalization by law, as many marginalized individuals took to graffiti as an avenue for identity expression. As Tricia Rose notes, graffiti has often been used as an expression of those individuals who otherwise belong to a marginalized group. Therefore, although "the writer credited with inspiring the movement, Taki 183, is a Greek teenager who lived in the Washington Heights section of Manhattan", Rose argues that "the vast majority of graffiti writers are black and Hispanic" (41-42). Graffiti, explains Rose, provided marginalized individuals a means for "claiming territories and inscribing their otherwise contained identities on public property" (22). The cultural rationale for graffiti, then, is that it offers a space for communicative bridges among marginalized communities separated by geographic space and simultaneously serves as an avenue for "disseminating [their] public performance" (Rose 43). In terming graffiti as a "public performance" in relation to otherwise marginalized identities, Rose suggests graffiti as an inadvertent rhetorical tactic that reaches the wider public through situating and circulating the writer's already raced, classed, and gendered identity, and subsequently their representative voice, into the space of the wider public where historically it has otherwise been underrepresented.

Although never strictly an issue of "juvenile delinquency," a discourse shift occurred with new policies that "reconstructed [graffiti] as a central reason for the decline in quality of life in a fiscally fragile and rusting New York" (Rose 44); graffiti was emblematic of an environment that was "uncontrolled and uncontrollable" (Glazer 4). Rose points out former Harvard Professor Nathan Glazer's 1979 article, "On Subway Graffiti in New York," which "argues that the significance of the graffiti 'problem' was in fact its symbolic power" (44). As Rose continues:

> According to Joe Austin and Craig Castleman, Glazer's 'out of control' rhetoric was instrumental in solidifying the image of graffiti writers as the source of New York's civic disorder and tarnished image, effectively displacing the more substantial and complex factors for New York's decline onto an unidentified band of black and Hispanic marauders. (Rose 44)

Here, Rose, along with Austin and Castleman, suggest that Glazer's notion of graffiti as "out of control" "symbolic power" is linked to the problem of whose symbolic power graffiti is attributed to (Rose 44). To be clear, this act of "civic disorder" is attributed not just to graffiti itself but the assumed identities of the writers (Rose 44). Rose suggests that graffiti became a symbol for marginalized voices, one that dominant ideologies sought to contain. Relatedly, approximately ten years after "Taki" was written, the work of African-American street-graffiti-writer-turned-gallery-artist, Jean-Michel Basquiat, was celebrated and raised to the level of culture (Rose 46). By shifting his work from graffiti and the everyday streets to high art and exclusive galleries, his political messages were simultaneously contained and commodified away from everyday circulation.

Anti-SB 1070 Graffiti

Scholars have discussed a rationale for gang-related graffiti (Cintron), gang graffiti as inner- and intra-related group discourse (Adams and Winter), and graffiti as a cultural expression of inner-city marginalized groups (Rose). That said, so far there has not been a detailed discussion placing graffiti as a rhetorical tradition spanning time and cultures, legitimizing it as a rhetorical tool against reductive notions of criminal acts and/or intentions. In addition, there has not been sufficient discourse on graffiti that connects the criminalization of graffiti with civic disorder and disobedience in connection to graffitists' assumed raced, classed, and gendered identities. That is, while graffiti has been an act carried out by bodies that are raced, classed, and gendered, it is the illegality of the act in accordance to the assumed identity of the graffitists that makes the act a transgression, where the act itself is often the result of a public sphere that sanctions some voices over others. Anti-SB 1070 graffiti provides an associative link between criminalized acts and criminalized bodies when those acts and bodies disrupt spaces and expose what it means to draw borders and make bodies and their attendant rhetorical tools illegal.

With acute marginalization of certain people in the public, especially those whose citizenship status is in question, it is reasonable to consider anti-SB 1070 graffiti as produced by those most affected by the bill. As Catherine Squires reminds us, when marginalized groups act in a public sphere in response to oppression, "[their] responses…emerge not only in reaction to oppression from the state or dominant public spheres, but also in relation to the internal politics of that particular public sphere and its material and cultural resources" (448). With a Latina/o population (illegal or otherwise) neither equally part of the discourse proceeding nor after the signing of an immigration bill targeted at their population—and with subsequent rhetorical moves to further marginalize the voice of this group, such as banning the teaching of ethnic studies in Arizona's K-12 classrooms (HB 2281)—anti-SB 1070 graffiti was a result of both the already existing marginalizing practices concerning civic engagement and the rhetorical avenues available as a result.

SB 1070 prompted plenty of graffiti, yet the way such work often circulated in public reflects how public spaces have civic borders that reflect appropriate spaces and forms of expression in relation to marginalized voices. For example, the anti-SB 1070 mural *We Are Human* created by Francisco Garcia, was part of a series of locally sanctioned murals, this one created in the back parking lot alley of Universal Hair Salon in Phoenix, Arizona (Lawton "Alley"), making such work confined to a limited space for circulation, raising the question of what local public(s) received this anti-SB 1070 dialogue.

Shortly after SB 1070 was signed into law, non-sanctioned graffiti was found in downtown Phoenix (Reynolds).

Figure 1: Garcia, Francisco. *We Are Human*

Unlike Garcia's sanctioned graffiti, this graffiti was, of course, anonymous. For purposes here I argue that it is the very anonymity of this illegal act of public transgression that

Figure 2: "Anti-SB 1070 Graffiti Popping Up in Downtown Phoenix"

most closely connects the issue of a bill on citizenship status to underlying issues of marginalized bodies and the circulation of their assumed representative rhetorics in the wider public. To be clear, it is the way that illegal rhetorical acts such as graffiti, which are now often associated with and carried out by bodies that are marginalized at intersecting forms of oppression, play upon the notion of citizenship status, where issues of legal/illegal rhetorical acts speak to marginalized bodies and their attendant discourses as already situated as illegal. In "The Fight Against SB 1070 and Why Graffiti Needs to be Involved," Matthew J notes the parallels "between the culture of graffiti and the citizens affected by...SB 1070," where "both entities are considered 'bad' by the mainstream ([graffitists] are called 'vandals' while migrants are dubbed 'illegal')... both [are] judged...on appearance..." (J). Although Matthew J calls for graffiti as an important form to use to "speak out against the bill," he also explains how "many 'big name' artists declined to be part of this project due to the fact that 'graffiti is not well respected' and any participation from our culture could, 'do more damage than good'" (J). Here, Matthew J's point reflects a public sphere that creates categorical differences among acceptable and unacceptable rhetorical tactics while simultaneously pushing some to use the unacceptable forms as available, creating a double bind for some, such as undocumented immigrants, who want to have a voice in the public sphere but face legal action if they do so, with or without graffiti as the rhetorical tool of choice.

Other than the photo from "Anti-SB 1070 Graffiti Popping Up in Downtown Phoenix," representative examples of anti-SB 1070 graffiti can be found only through the ABC 15 Arizona TV newscast redistributed on Jay Reynolds' written online coverage of the issue. The newscast explains that these "[anti-SB 1070] messages are showing up on everything from stop signs to a mural on the side of a building" (Reynolds). Examples include the words "No More Police State" sprayed in dark paint on the back of a sign, and a black stencil that reads "1070" below the word "STOP" on a stop sign. While the graffiti was produced just months after SB 1070 was made into law, Reynolds' media coverage only minimally nods to anti-SB 1070 graffiti as a protest tactic. Instead, Reynolds' interview with Chiara Elie, manager of Alta Lofts in downtown Phoenix, a building affected by graffiti, focuses on the effects of graffiti on the property values of this downtown loft residence. Elie does make one comment about SB 1070 when she argues that anti-SB 1070 protesting voices can be carried out in ways other than graffiti (Reynolds). Here, Elie inadvertently emphasizes the double bind of the wider public sphere that would both dismiss the rationale behind such graffiti as a rhetorical tactic, and elide the fact that the undocumented have often been tied to a capitalist economy with illegal immigrants either adding or taking away from the system (Beltrán 597), which the Alta Lofts in Phoenix perhaps represent.

In *Angels' Town*, Ralph Cintron explores the various ways that the marginalized Latina/o population in his study vie for "respect under conditions of little or no respect" (164) to include graffiti produced by and for local Latina/o gang members. As Cintron explains, graffiti proves to be "an important narrative 'tactic' available to gang members for the public expression of their subjectivities [which are] constantly being suppressed by the public sphere" (176). Of course, for Cintron it is not about promoting gang activity or locating such activity as either the only or specifically Latina/o response to oppression, but rather he considers how this activity and its attendant rhetorics are avenues of resistance to practices that simultaneously marginalize through geographic, economic, and civic isolation. For Cintron, the act of gang graffiti signals a way to "claim metaphorical ownership (or, to use one of the street terms, "rulership") over public spaces" (175). This "ownership" is part of a "shadow system" that, as a tactic, mimics the system world through partial appropriation, while separating itself from such systems (Cintron 175). Elenore Long explains that "in mimicking the mainstream culture, or system world, the shadow system protects the difference between itself and the system world, and claims this difference as its identity" (137). Finding a safe space for identity formation and expression in the wider public is certainly a dilemma for those whose public status hinges on documented citizenship. In this sense, anti-SB 1070 political graffiti can be understood to be working from the position of a shadow system as it both "mimics" the ways discourses are circulated across publics as well as shelters its identity by exploiting the difference between dominant discourses and those that are otherwise marginalized.

This shadow tactic is important, for part of the double bind faced by marginalized groups whose citizenship status and subsequent rights to equity in civic engagement is at issue is that certain tactics risk reifying problematic assimilation narratives, countering calls for equity. This is Cristina Beltrán's point when she notes how one result of the 2006 immigration reform marches was that both pro- and anti-immigration discourse linked Latina/o citizenship with laboring bodies, whereby re-inscribing Latina/o citizenship status according to labor and thus economic capital. Beltrán states that "By taking to the streets and claiming space and rights, immigrants and their allies created relational spaces of freedom and common appearance where none existed before" (597). Yet, as Beltrán points out:

> Lacking from both [pro- and anti-immigration] accounts was virtually any recognition or appreciation of the profoundly political character of the events of 2006. When faced with the extraordinary and unanticipated fact of noncitizen mass protest, both pro- and anti-immigrant forces tended to shift the focus away from the unexpected quality of these activities, reverting to more recognizable discussions of legalization, naturalization, and employment. (597)

Here, assimilation, or "membership," and thus citizenship is constructed as constitutive of labor contributions, so while pro-immigration activists were unwittingly contributing to the notion of the potentially exploitive nature of Latina/o labor, anti-immigration activists were perpetuating the image of this group as an "ever-growing economic and cultural threat" (Beltrán 596-597). With this in mind, anti-SB 1070 graffiti suggests a discourse move against appeals to citizenship through assimilation. And, such work should also be understood to be different than the more defiant and closed-to-the-wider-public tactical system found in Cintron's discussion of gang-related graffiti. While anti-SB 1070 graffiti can be understood to be a tactic that mimics the system world, unlike gang graffiti, such a tactic seeks out discourse with the larger public as opposed to serving as a closed dialogue system produced and read by members only. This follows the point made by Karen L. Adams and Anne Winter whose research on gang graffiti in Phoenix, Arizona argues that such acts are "about membership in a group" where gang members address each other as well as those in rival gangs to "reinforc[e] their reality" (341). Group solidarity is certainly an inherent part of any type of graffiti that draws attention to issues of belonging in relation to groups affected by intersecting forms of oppression. However, gang graffiti closes itself off from the larger public, whereas political graffiti, such as that related to anti-SB 1070, suggests a direct move to produce dialogue with the wider public. This is because gang graffiti is difficult to read for outsiders of that community (Adams and Winter 341). In contrast, the very nature of political graffiti is that it is to be read across publics—political graffiti demands the attention of wider publics in ways that gang graffiti only indirectly does. One aspect that does connect gang-related graffiti with the more overt acts of public dialogue inherent in political graffiti is that, similar to Cintron's analysis, these acts have a socially situated rationale, and therefore I argue should be considered a rhetorical tool worthy of further exploration as both emblematic of and used by otherwise silenced voices.

Graffiti and the Dominant Public Sphere

To understand both the rhetorical rationale and function of graffiti, it is important to consider how the dominant public sphere functions at the level of everyday practices. There are two levels in which to understand the public sphere. On one hand, the public sphere can be understood as a literal place of discourse. Here I follow Catherine Squires' definition of the public sphere as "a set of physical or mediated spaces where people can gather and share information, debate opinions, and tease out their political interests and social needs with other participants" (448). On the other hand, the public sphere can be understood as actual physical or geographic spaces that often normatively, albeit invisibly, serve as a discourse canvas or landscape. This in part follows Henri Lefebvre's argument that physical or abstract space is "inherently political" (Brenner and Elden 358). What connects the public sphere of both Squires and Lefebvre is that both are normalized in their production and circulation of situated knowledges and rhetorics. This is Fraser's point concerning the public sphere of discourse that is normalized as white, middle-class, and male (113-114; Squires 450). Concerning abstract space, Neil Brenner and Stuart Elden explain Lefebvre's "'territory effect'—the state's tendency, through its territorial form, to naturalize (at once to mask and to normalize) its own transformative, intensely patterning effects upon sociospatial relations" (354). Specifically, Brenner and Elden conclude that "while the political illusion of transparency permeates all dimensions of state space..., it is tied in particularly central ways to territory, which may be viewed as its site *par excellence* (372). As a function of the state and therefore part of the dominant public, the "territory effect" can be understood as public space that is inherently politically patterned to represent and foster white, middle-class, and male voices.

Further, public spaces circulate discourses that demand our public attention, working on us consciously or otherwise. As Michael Warner points out, "Your attention is everywhere solicited by artifacts" that call for an audience (7). Warner sets the study of "publics" against the larger more ephemeral backdrop of "the public" to demonstrate that there is no "one" public, but rather a set of text-based circulating discourses that are organized as a body (68). Warner observes that publics are called into being by self-address. "'Run it up a flagpole, and see who salutes,'" he muses (114). What the self-reflexivity of a public means for the study of graffiti is that dominant discourses circulate by the very nature of texts. However, political graffiti creates a space of dialogue that inserts itself into the otherwise normative dominant discourse of the public sphere. Squires explains how marginalized groups, "people of color, women, homosexuals, religious minorities, and immigrant groups have created coexisting counterpublics in reaction to the exclusionary politics of dominant public spheres and the state" (446). Such exclusionary measures necessitate different responses or rhetorical tactics based on "given existing political, economic, social, and cultural conditions" (Squires 448). This follows Long's point on how Warner's discourse of "poetic world making" means that marginalized groups "formulate oppositional identities, alternative discourse, and competing worldviews..., resisting the exclusionary norms of rational-critical discourse and creating a space for performative world making" (249). The poetic world making of political graffiti works to disrupt the otherwise normative circulation of the dominant public sphere in such unassuming physical public spaces, where this disruption points to the presence of these spaces as normative while simultaneously pointing to the absence of marginalized rhetorics.

Political graffiti, then, disrupts everyday publics by use of topoi. As Long notes, "topoi are the commonplaces through which ideology structures the interpretive landscape of a given location, creating 'a very tight knot of emotion, reality, and ideological interpretation'" (Cintron qtd. in Long 138). By disrupting the everyday topoi of the physical public landscape, political graffiti "invoke[s] simultaneously both itself (counter discourse and absence of voices) as well as the opposite (a dominant public sphere discourse that is normalized in the everyday)" (Long 138). Taking off from Habermas' notion of the public sphere, Cintron states:

> Within the restricted public sphere, not even contesting parties represent the entire realm of contestation that cycles throughout a society. The breadth and depth of contestation does not become aired partly because not all the varied voices have been certified, sometimes literally, to speak in such a public sphere. (175)

While political graffiti is not the only tactic used by those whose voices are marginalized to one degree or another in the public sphere, the rationale for such acts can be understood to correspond to the ways in which marginalized voices are often afforded little capital, often do not circulate to wider publics, and are undervalued in terms of civic engagement. The overture of political graffiti does the dual work of both elevating such voices into the circulation of a wider public as well as pointing to the fact that such voices are devalued. By marking public spaces, political graffiti questions who owns public spaces, and thus who and what belongs in such spaces.

Moreau and Alderman argue how anti-graffiti rhetoric carried out by institutions or organizations such as Graffiti Hurts "seeks to justify the erasure of graffiti, and in so doing it reinforces exclusionary representations of culture, community, and landscape" (106). More specifically, "Organizations such as Graffiti Hurts play a critical and often unquestioned role in not only vilifying graffitists but also justifying broader, exclusionary ideas about political identity and what counts for citizenship" (Moreau and Alderman 121). I wish to expand on this point made by Moreau and Alderman. Anti-SB 1070 graffiti not only challenges the exclusion of certain groups as part of the discourse of the public sphere, but also links the criminalization of bodies that are "othered" (immigrants) with the criminalization of graffiti as an act of civic disorder. More precisely, the illegalization of bodies in tandem with the illegalization of graffiti as an unrecognized or criminalized rhetorical tool prompts questions about what I call *civic disobedience* in relation to who is legal or authorized—whose voice counts—as a citizen in the larger public.

Gloria Anzaldúa explains, "Borders are set up to define the places that are safe and unsafe, to distinguish *us* from *them*"(25). As a law about territorial borders, SB 1070 naturalizes both literal and ideological spaces as a divide between citizen and noncitizen. The privatization of the public sphere as a space for civic engagement goes beyond constitutional categories of legal and illegal citizenship, moving towards nativism and the ownership of both ideological and literal-physical spaces. In a system closed to counter-discourse and supported by nativist ideology, how might graffiti, an undervalued and criminalized act, cleave open a rhetorical space of cross-public engagement?

Conclusion

In "The Space for Rhetoric in Everyday Life," John Ackerman uses Henri Lefebvre's spatial theory, where social space is "'both a field of action...and a basis of action'" (Lefebvre qtd. in Ackerman 86), to argue the value of exploring the rhetorical nature of social spaces, or "sites," as such "spaces are the result of someone's design and rendering" (86). While Ackerman's focus is on architecture and the creation and existence of social sites (91), his call to "extend our fluency in rhetorical situations and agency in order to address the historical and material attributes of social space and everyday life" (85) can be applied to the study of graffiti as a rhetorical tactic. Graffiti exists, of course, in social spaces that are already constructed architectural and/or geographical sites, and therefore graffiti can be understood to be a response to these constructions. Thus, similar to Ackerman's call to bring lived spaces into the discourse of "rhetoric, composition, and literacy" studies (85), here I have argued for graffiti to be given recognition and importance as a rhetorical tactic worthy of study.

How we, as scholars, go about such study has its own complications. For of course, it can be argued that a study of political graffiti and marginalized voices can further complicate the position of these groups when graffiti is understood as a criminalized act. Yet, while such work can complicate already vulnerable identities, it does so largely because of the way graffiti is situated as a criminal act without a rationale and absent of rhetorical meaning outside this view. Lorraine Higgins, Elenore Long and Linda Flower state that "rhetorically grounded community literacy opens up a unique space where intercultural partners can inquire into and deliberate about problems, working toward both personal and public change" (10). This type of intercultural inquiry is often a space that needs to be created, for as Linda Flower explains, "A public (like a community) is constructed, not found—a symbolic space that comes into being when issues of mutual concern call people into existence as a public, and some people accept the invitation" (3-4). If spaces need to be created, there needs to be some cue for opening up intercultural dialogue. Yet, in privatized discourse spaces, spaces for intercultural inquiry are not readily made, which is why I argue for community literacy scholars and those interested in engaging the public through cross-cultural dialogue give importance to political graffiti as a rhetorical tool. Through a consideration of *rhetorical listening* and cultural logics in relation to normative assumptions of public spaces and rhetorical acts, the final point of argument here is to consider rhetorically listening to our assumptions about graffiti, and in doing so, to cleave a space for engaging graffiti as a rhetorical tool worthy of exploration. To be clear, I seek here to connect Ratcliffe's work on rhetorical listening with the role that scholars in community literacy and social activists might play in directing attention to graffiti as a rhetorical tool. Recognition and discourse on graffiti as a rhetorical tool can aid in bringing the rationale behind political graffiti into the very public dialogue that these acts seek, creating the potential for fostering cross-public engagement; a site for considering the "commonalities and differences" that shape identities and identifications (Ratcliffe 32), as much as their attendant rhetorical tools (Squires 448).

Works Cited

Ackerman, John. "The Space for Rhetoric in Everyday Life." *Towards a Rhetoric of Everyday Life: New Directions in Research on Writing, Text, and Discourse*. Ed. Martin Nystrand and John Duffy. Madison: U of Wisconsin P, 2003. 84-117. Print.

"ACLU Demands Removal of Detainees from Arizona Immigration Detention Center." Immigrant Rights. American Civil Liberties Union of Arizona. 12 June 2012. Web. 16 Feb. 2013.

Adams, Karen L. and Anne Winter. "Gang Graffiti as a Discourse Genre." *Journal of Sociolinguistics*. 1.3 (1997): 337-360. Print.

Anzaldúa, Gloria. *Borderlands / La Frontera: The New Mestiza*. 2nd ed. San Francisco: Aunt Lute, 1999. Print.

"Arizona's Immigration Enforcement Laws." Prepared by Ann Morse. Immigration. *National Conference of State Legislatures*. 8 July 2011. Web. 17 May 2012.

Baird, J. A. "The Graffiti of Dura-Europos: A Contextual Approach." *Ancient Graffiti in Context*. Ed. J.A. Baird and Claire Taylor. New York: Routledge, 2011. 49-68. Print.

Baird, J.A., and Claire Taylor. "Preface." *Ancient Graffiti in Context*. Ed. J.A. Baird and Claire Taylor. New York: Routledge, 2011. xv. Print.

———. "Ancient Graffiti in Context: Introduction." *Ancient Graffiti in Context*. Ed. J.A. Baird and Claire Taylor. New York: Routledge, 2011. 1-19. Print.

Beltrán, Cristina. "Going Public: Hannah Arendt, Immigrant Action, and the Space of Appearance." *Political Theory*. 37.5 (2009): 595-622. Print.

Benefiel, Rebecca R. "Dialogues of Graffiti in the House of the Four Styles at Pompeii (*Casa Dei Quattro Stili*, I.8.17, 11)." *Ancient Graffiti in Context*. Ed. J.A. Baird and Claire Taylor. New York: Routledge, 2011. 20-48. Print.

Brenner, Neil, and Stuart Elden. "Henri Lefebvre on State, Space, Territory." *International Political Sociology*. 3.4 (2009): 353-377. Print.

Brewer, Janice. "Statement by Governor on SB 1070." Office of the Governor. Phoenix, AZ. 23 April 2010. Web. 17 May 2012. Transcript.

Cintron, Ralph. *Angels' Town: Chero Ways, Gang Life, and the Rhetorics of the Everyday*. Boston: Beacon, 1997. Print.
Flower, Linda. *Community Literacy and the Rhetoric of Public Engagement*. Carbondale: SIU P, 2008. Print.
Fraser, Nancy. "Rethinking the Public Sphere: A Contribution to the Critique of Actually Existing Democracy." *Habermas and the Public Sphere*. Ed. Craig Calhoun. Cambridge: MIT P, 1992. 109-142. Print.
Garcia, Francisco. *We Are Human*. 2010. Phoenix, AZ.
Glazer, Nathan. "On Subway Graffiti in New York." *Public Interest*. 54 (1979): 3-11. Proquest. 2001. Web. 6 June 2012.
Habermas, Jürgen. *The Structural Transformation of the Public Sphere: An Inquiry into a Category of Bourgeois Society*. Cambridge: MIT P, 1991. Print.
Higgins, Lorraine, Elenore Long, and Linda Flower. "Community Literacy: A Rhetorical Model for Personal and Public Inquiry." *Community Literacy Journal*. 1.1 (2006): 9-43. Print.
J., Matthew. "The Fight Against SB 1070 and Why Graffiti Needs To Be Involved." *Bombing Science*.Web. 20 Feb. 2013.
Lawton, Claire. "Alley Tour: Grand Avenue and Polk Street." Blogs: Mural City. Phoenix New Times. 29 Oct. 2010. Web. 14 Feb. 2013
Long, Elenore. *Community Literacy and the Rhetoric of Local Publics*. West Lafayette: Parlor Press, 2008. Print.
Moreau, Terri and Derek H. Alderman. "Graffiti Hurts and the Eradication of Alternative Landscape Expression." *The Geographical Review*. 101.1 (2011): 106-124. Print.
Ratcliffe, Krista. *Rhetorical Listening: Identification, Gender, Whiteness*. Carbondale, SIU Press, 2005. Print.
Reynolds, Jay. "Anti-SB 1070 Graffiti Popping Up in Downtown Phoenix." *ABC 15.com*. 2 Aug. 2010. Web. 8 Nov. 2011.
Rose, Tricia. *Black Noise: Rap Music and Black Culture in Contemporary America*. Hanover: Wesleyan UP, 1994. Music Online: *African American Music Reference*. Alexander Street Press, LLC. Web. 6 June 2012.
Sexton, Connie Cone, et al. "Thousands March in Phoenix to Protest Immigration Law". *The Arizona Republic*. 29 May 2010. Web. 23 May 2012.
Squires, Catherine R. "Rethinking the Black Public Sphere: An Alternative Vocabulary for Multiple Public Spheres." *Communication Theory*. 12.4 (2002): 446-468. Print.
"Stop SB 1070- We Will Not Comply' Civil Disobedience Outside Courthouse." News and Updates. Alto Arizona. n.d. Web. 18 Jan. 2012.
"'Taki 183' Spawns Pen Pals." New York Times. 21 July 1971:37. *ProQuest Historical Newspapers: The New York Times (1851-2008)*. Web. 17 May 2012.
Wagner, Dennis. "Violence Is Not Up on Arizona Border: Mexico Crime Flare, but Here, Only Flickers." *The Arizona Republic*. 22 May 2010. Web. 17 May 2012.
Warner, Michael. *Publics and Counterpublics*. Brooklyn: Zone Books, 2005. Print.

Wessler, Seth Freed. "Bills Modeled After Arizona's SB 1070 Spread through States." *Colorlines*. 2 March 2011. Web. 17 May 2012.

Young, Iris Marion. *Inclusion and Democracy*. New York: Oxford UP, 2000. Print.

Zadorojnyi, Alexei V. "Transcripts of Dissent? Political Graffiti and Elite Ideology Under the Principate." *Ancient Graffiti in Context*. Ed. J.A. Baird and Claire Taylor. New York: Routledge, 2011. 110-133. Print.

Author Bio

Veronica Oliver is a PhD candidate at Arizona State University. Her dissertation studies the construction and public circulation of argumentative appeals in relation to an activist organization's decision-making that attempts to leverage its identity and membership both to serve its constituents and to continue to direct wider public attention to a public controversy. To document the complexity of this decision-making, the study grounds its analysis in the rhetorical work of Puente Arizona, a grassroots organization made of mixed-documentation status residents responding to Senate Bill 1070, recent legislation aimed at deterring illegal immigration and deporting current undocumented residents in Arizona. She has recently published an article in *Reflections: A Journal of Public Rhetoric, Civic Writing, and Service Learning*.

Book & New Media Reviews

From the Book Review Editor's Desk

Jessica Shumake, with editorial support from Jim Bowman (St. John Fisher College)
Georgia College and State University

Anthony D. Boynton, II and Saul Hernandez, Interns
Georgia College and State University

As my upper division rhetoric and English majors share the critical theory statements they've written as a preamble to each class, I'm keenly aware that our Literary Theory course has taken *Literacy* Theory as the main focus. When one student argues that, in order for something to be considered literary, it must somehow seek to transform the world and redress power imbalances, other students move into the strongly agree or disagree corners of the room for a spirited debate. If the measure of an artifact's literariness is that it makes a gesture toward the goal of social change, how big of a gesture must change-oriented projects make? As the debate unfolds, one question that emerges is whether or not a fast food kids' meal book about healthy eating might qualify as more *literary* than an established masterwork like *Finnegans Wake*. Some are more moved by the pragmatic potential of the children's book, while others argue that Joyce's innovative prose opens radical possibilities for breaking with established narrative conventions. Does the children's book do more to extend literacy than Joyce's masterpiece? Perhaps it does. Debate participants ultimately decide that both texts are valuable, though they are legitimated differently in different communities, which complicates often-dichotomized terms such as "vernacular culture" and "high culture." The suggestion here is that respect and productive interaction can occur across divergent sites and literacy practices.

The circulation of texts, agency, power, ideas, and resources is a thematic constant in the texts and reviews in this issue. William Carney's keywords essay on *critical service learning* sets the tone for the book reviews that follow, as he explores the inequalities and power imbalances at play in our most earnest and "unapologetic" attempts to enact social change as literacy educators. Carney suggests that students' written reflections on service-learning partnerships, even when those partnerships may strike us as failures, can meet the more modest goal of helping students to understand better literacy work as more than just the teaching of reading, writing, and workplace skills. The example Carney gives is a service-learning project wherein writing tutors, who were also full-time undergraduate students, grew to better understand the lives of the community members they worked with even though the tutors couldn't ultimately offer the intensive English instruction the community members desired.

David Dadurka's review of *The Unheard Voices: Community Organizations and Service Learning* explores how service-learning partnerships can be better designed to address community members' needs and perspectives in sustainable ways. Dadurka's review calls attention to three essential principles of successful and reciprocal relationships: commitment, communication, and compatibility. He reasons that the principles may help to offset the tendency of members of educational institutions to position themselves as more privileged or knowledgeable than the community members with whom they work. As Dadurka emphasizes, "commitment may be the most fundamental" principle because it is essential to the maintenance of good communication and the "will to develop training and screening mechanisms to assure compatibility."

In Beth Savoy's review of *Circulating Communities: The Tactics and Strategies of Community Publishing*, it is apparent that the *community* aspect of the community publishing process is even more important than the products made. Savoy's review showcases the book's divergent array of community publishing projects. These projects share in common the aim of challenging "dominant, mainstream media" perspectives to position community members as valuable producers of knowledge. The importance of cultivating rhetorical tactics and strategies to resist dominant ideologies also comes to the fore in Jenna Vinson's dynamic review of Adela Licona's *Zines in Third Space: Radical Cooperation and Borderlands Rhetoric*. As Vinson suggests, zines (often collaborative, self-published magazines) provide cultural workers a space to situate rhetoric as a practice that's adaptable to specific communities and real-world exigencies.

In terms of pragmatic needs, when a student of mine pursuing a career as a high school teacher, expresses enthusiasm for *Pedagogy of the Oppressed* and asks me where she could learn more about the complications of applying Freirean methods to the classroom, I am grateful to be able to recommend Katie Sylvester and Anne-Marie Hall's review of Lesley Bartlett's book *The Word and the World*. Sylvester and Hall use a dialogue format to discuss "the deeply ideological implications of the work we do as literacy educators." They frame their discussion around 1) Bartlett's view on the limitations of Freirean praxis; 2) the complicated emotions and destructive myths and assumptions that are ever-present in community literacy work; and 3) why Bartlett's ethnographic research is particularly relevant to community literacy specialists who seek global and comparative perspectives on literacy education.

Critical Service Learning

William Carney
Cameron University

Keyword Essay

Service learning has become a feature in higher education in courses ranging from computer science and graphic design to English and the humanities. These courses are designed to provide "internship" experience and enable students to use skills they learned in the classroom in "real world settings." These "real world settings," however, exist in some rather well-defined economic, social, and political system. Tania Mitchell suggests that traditional approaches to service learning either assume that such projects are already inherently related to social justice or are simply concerned with other issues such as the teaching of some rather acontextual "workplace skills." There exists, however, a growing recognition that service learning could enable students to recognize and more deeply understand the social and economic structures they are asked to work within. The aims of this "critical service-learning" approach include the redistribution of power in the service-learning relationship, the development of authentic relationships between the university and community, and an unapologetic movement toward the goal of social change. At my university there is an interest in providing service learning in more traditional workplace settings, but there are also faculty members who are attempting to use these projects to help students understand the contexts in which they live and work. This keywords essay details some recent scholarship in literacy and critical service learning. It is by no means a complete picture of the efforts in this area but, rather, presents some interesting service-learning projects that might be duplicated at other institutions. All the projects provide opportunities for students to gain an understanding of the economic, social, political, and, in one case, environmental contexts in which they live. Writing plays a primary role in facilitating such understanding.

Lisa Rabin's article "The Culmore Bilingual ESL and Popular Education Project: Coming to Consciousness on Labor, Literacy, and Community," details a service-learning project featured in a Spanish class at George Mason University. The project offered an alternative to more "market-based" service learning. In 2009, Rabin had been contacted by labor organizers from the Tenants and Workers United (TWU) in Culmore, Virginia to possibly have some of her bilingual students offer an ESL course for day laborers who were also new immigrants at the union's offices. A former graduate student of Rabin's was asked to spearhead the project and train the undergraduates who would serve as ESL teachers. The project attempted to build a bridge between academic literacy and community literacy using the "popular education" model (Calderon 2006). Rabin deemed the summer-long project a failure. She noted that the clients of the program needed intensive Basic English instruction, a job that was much too large for full-time undergraduate students. The "separateness" between the two groups remained. The course, however, met a smaller goal, providing the opportunity for undergraduate students in a Spanish course to consider the role of structural forces in creating and sustaining inequity in Latino/a neighborhoods. Indeed, half of the undergraduate students were themselves "heritage" speakers of Spanish who grew up in bilingual households. Although Rabin was disappointed by what she considered the failure of the project to make positive changes in the lives of its clients, the undergraduate tutors seemed to come to a better understanding of the lives of immigrant day laborers. The sort of critical service-learning that students engaged in provided a more visceral understanding of the socioeconomic barriers at work in Hispanic neighborhoods. She suggests that service learning projects are too often hijacked by market entities that impose a neoliberal ideology on the very necessary work students perform. In Rabin's project, students were able to form an attachment with the neighborhood where the clients lived and worked. This sort of service-learning project offers literacy services to clients while providing students a different lens through which to view their experiences.

Similarly, in the journal *Reading Improvement*, Janet C. Richards explores how participation in a service-learning project might impact the professional dispositions of graduate education majors. Specifically, she wanted to know if participation in such a project would impact the majors' attitudes toward and competence in teaching students of color. Twenty-eight predominantly white graduate students collaboratively taught a writing strategies course in a community center in a low-income housing area. The K-5 students they worked with had all scored at or below the 20th percentile on a battery of standardized writing and reading measures. The reflective writing that the graduate students were asked to do followed some interesting patterns. At first, a sense of frustration with both the K-5 students as well as with the collaborative aspect of the project was the primary focus of the writing. As the project continued, however, students began to consider the "relational" aspects of their work. They also started to write in detail about the relationship between their work and bigger issues of social justice. Specifically, a number of the graduate students considered how their teaching would be performed within the existing political structure of a school, a school district, and larger social systems. Students were, thus, able to understand that classroom teaching occurs in some clearly-defined, although not always visible contexts.

Christine Greenhow describes another approach to service-learning pedagogy in her article, "Online Social Networks and Learning." Greenhow, a Professor of Education and Information Studies at the University of Maryland, discusses the use of social media outlets as sites for literacy learning. While most school districts see Facebook as a distractor for students, Greenhow suggests that online social networking can stimulate social and civic benefits, online and offline, which has positive implications for education. She argues that "social capital," which she defines as the resources or benefits available to people through their interactions that creates feelings of trust, reciprocity and social cohesion, and places the creation of networks as the primary focus of venues for learning. She suggests that, although many school districts place limits or impose outright bans on social media during the school day, these sites are a large part of students' learning "ecology." Indeed, their ubiquity would indicate that ignoring the power of these sites makes little sense for educators. Instead, Greenhow asks that we consider how "offers of practical, just-in-time assistance, information, emotional or psychological aid, modeling, coaching," all features of social media, can be used (9). Limits on the use of social media outlets seem ill-informed, as these are the sites of communication that students find most meaningful. Indeed, bans or limits seem only to lead to student resistance. She proposes using Facebook and other social media sites as the venues for service learning in literacy tutoring.

A credit-bearing required information literacy course became the site of a service-learning course at Wright State University (2011). Maureen Barry, a librarian there, developed a service-learning project that served the Children's Hunger Alliance (CHA) in Ohio. Roughly 500,000 children in that state are food insecure, or don't know where or when they will find their next meal. The CHA partners with schools, child-care providers, faith-based organizations, and other youth-serving nonprofits to increase USDA child nutrition program participation and relieve food insecurity. Students in the course fulfilled the components of the service-learning project in two ways: first, they served at after-school programs that promote nutrition and physical activity, and second, they supplied research portfolios to CHA staff members. As they picked out useful topics to help CHA improve child nutrition, students discover parts of the World Wide Web considered invisible (i.e., the dark web) to the general public. They are guided in their search by the expressed needs to the CHA and by what they experience themselves in their work at the after-school programs. Course outcomes indicate that the dual experiences of work in the after-school programs and information literacy activities create a sense of empowerment for students (i.e., that research and literacy can change peoples' situations for the better). The course activities also serve to create a better bond between university students and the larger community. The program continues and the research has enabled CHA to expand its program offerings.

An article by Jason F. Lovvorn, Linda Holt, and Charmion Gustke, "Service-Learning Liberations: Transformation through Personal Writing, Community Partnership, and Student Advocacy" published in the *Belmont Humanities Symposium Journal* explores not only the services provided in three projects by undergraduate students but also the type of writing they do to record and make sense of their experiences. Students in one project, members of a junior-level class in literacy, spent the semester working with clients at the Nashville Adult Literacy Council. The reflective writing these students composed for the course was comprised of first-person narratives. These narrative writing assignments provided a venue through which students could connect their experiences with the course content. In another project, students worked in a community garden project for a parolee halfway house. The personal writing that these students did was transformative in that it enabled them to consider issues of race and class. The writing in these two cases was an integral part of the projects, allowing students a space in which to develop an understanding of various types of literacy and how these literacies support or subvert systems of economic, social, and racial privilege.

Scientific literacy was the focus of a service-learning project by Julie Reynolds and Jennifer Ahern-Dodson. They wanted to design a course that would increase science literacy, help students understand scientific inquiry, improve writing skills, and learn about local environmental concerns. The Eno River in North Carolina was the site of the project and students wrote collaboratively about the connections they gleaned between what they learned in their introductory science class and what they observed near and in the river. The project has led to external grant funding for future efforts but, according to the authors, the real reward from the project involved student learning and students coming to understand their roles as environmental stewards. A number of the students have been inspired to continue this work after the course was completed.

Service learning provides great value to a student's educational experience. As a variety of active learning, it can teach skills in ways that classroom practice alone cannot. But, without clearly defined pedagogical goals, service learning serves to reinforce hierarchies of class and gender. Too often it seems to impart the message to students that "this is the way things are." Yet, if students are encouraged to explore things such as class structure, organizational hierarchies and power, environmental degradation, access and ability, race, and gender, these concepts take on new meaning and can be understood in some very profound new ways. The service-learning course can become transformational rather than simply a conduit for the transmission of information and skill. The articles discussed here all represent examples of critical service learning. In these projects, students are encouraged to learn about the immigrant experience, barriers to literacy for students of color, appropriate educational goals for social media, food insecurity, incarceration, and environmental problems. Writing becomes the means through which students make the connections between what they learn in the classroom and what they experience. Many projects are replicable in different university classrooms and communities and all encourage a deeper understanding of structural inequalities.

Works Cited

Barry, Maureen. "Research for the greater good Incorporating service learning in an information Literacy course at Wright State University." *College & Research Libraries News* 72.6 (2011): 345-348.

Calderon, Jose Z., Suzanne F. Foster, and Silvia L. Rodriguez. "Organizing immigrant workers: Action research and strategies in the Pomona Day Labor Center." *Latino Los Angeles: Transformations, Communities, and Activism*. U Arizona P. 278-99, 2005.

Carney, William. "'Welcome to Oklahoma': A Service-Learning Project in an Undergraduate Technical Writing Course." *Sino-US English Teaching* 9.9 (2012): 1451-1456. Web.

Greenhow, Christine. "Online Social Networks and Learning." *On the Horizon* 19.1 (2011): 4-12.

Lovvorn, Jason F., Linda Holt, and Charmion Gustke. "Service-Learning Liberations: Transformation through Personal Writing, Community Partnership, and Student Advocacy. *Belmont Humanities Symposium Journal 2* (2011): 116-34.

Mitchell, Tania D. "Traditional vs. Critical Service-Learning: Engaging the Literature to Differentiate Two Models." *Michigan Journal of Community Service Learning* 14.2 (2008): 50-65.

Rabin, Lisa M. "The Culmore Bilingual ESL and Popular Education Project: Coming to Consciousness on Labor, Literacy, and Community." *Radical Teacher* 91.1 (2011): 58-67.

Reynolds, Julie A., and Jennifer Ahern-Dodson. "Promoting Science Literacy through Research Service-Learning—An Emerging Pedagogy with Significant Benefits for Students, Faculty, Universities, and Communities." *Journal of College Science Teaching* 39.6 (2010): 24-29.

Richards, Janet C. "Transformations in Graduate Education Majors' Relational Care in a Service-Learning Writing Course." *Reading Improvement* 50.1 (2013): 19-29. Web.

The Unheard Voices: Community Organizations and Service Learning
Randy Stoecker, Elizabeth A. Tryon, with Amy Hilgendorf
Philadelphia: Temple UP, 2009. 232 pp.

Reviewed by David Dadurka
University of Central Florida

An extensive field report about community organizations in the greater Madison, WI, region, *The Unheard Voices* offers a rare look into how charities and nonprofit organizations perceive their service-learning relationships with academic institutions. From the perspective of community partners, the view isn't always so pleasant. *The Unheard Voices* fills a frequently ignored gap in service-learning studies and offers long overdue insight from community partners. However, the book's value is limited by its focus solely on the Madison region, an area known for its community activism and service-learning participation. Despite this limitation, the book is effective at raising awareness about the level of sustained engagement needed by both academics and community partners to create greater reciprocity in service-learning projects.

The volume's editors Randy Stoecker, Elizabeth A. Tryon, and Amy Hilgendorf, all based out of the University of Wisconsin-Madison, note that despite service learning's goal of serving community partners, service-learning researchers have generally ignored the perspective of those organizations that academic institutions aim to serve (5). Stoecker, Tryon, and Hilgendorf start with the premise that there are problems inherent with doing service learning from the "perspective of the academy" (viii) and ask the question "Who is served by service learning?" (1). Using responses from sixty-seven interviews with staff of community organizations in the greater Madison region, the authors' results suggest that higher education institutions appear to reap more of the rewards of service-learning partnerships than community organizations.

The book itself emerges from a service-learning project, born of a graduate seminar on qualitative research in which both graduate and undergraduate students—with a wide range of backgrounds in nonprofit work—contributed to the majority of the book chapters. This model itself suggests what service-learning practitioners might undertake in their communities to improve the effectiveness of service projects, and it represents one of the greatest strengths of the book.

The first half of the book (chapters one through five) is devoted to understanding the problems with service-learning relationships, the motivations that drive community organizations to participate in service learning, how they engage in partnerships and manage service learners. The second half (chapters six through ten) develops responses to address the problems that drive community partners away from service-learning partnerships.

In chapter one, Stoecker and Tryon highlight the growing concern over the "issue of whether service learning truly serves communities" (3). The authors argue that previous research has been based on "superficial" methods, using focus groups and Likert scale questionnaires to present a rosy picture of community organization and educational institution service-learning relationships (5). They argue that projects, because educational institutions are the main drivers of them, have veered too far to the learning side of service learning, ignoring the service aspects and what benefits the community reaps from such relationships. Stoecker draws on his twenty years of experience to highlight instances of disengaged faculty who sometimes don't care about the results of unsuccessful community projects, fail to manage service learners, or lack understanding of the needs of their partner organizations or local communities.

Chapter two provides an overview of what motivates community organizations to participate in service learning. Authors Shannon Bell and Rebecca Carlson assert four primary reasons community organizations work with service learners: to build capacity, to achieve long-term education goals, to form potentially advantageous relationships with the university community, and to help students better understand their work. While building capacity seems intuitive for community organizations, Bell and Carlson point out that they were "greatly surprised to learn that many community organizations hosted service learners not because it expanded organizational capacity, but because the organizational staff saw it as part of their mission to educate the public" (23). However, Bell and Carlson end the chapter with a quote from a community partner who notes that putting students to work with meaningful, education-focused tasks as opposed to busy work like "photocopying" requires an investment of time that many nonprofits are not staffed or trained to address.

Chapter three discusses the various ways community organizations recruit volunteers and service learners. Authors Cassandra Garcia, Sarah Nehrling, Amy Martin, and Kristy SeBlonka note that researchers "know amazingly little about this question" (38). The majority of interviewees considered volunteer fairs as an ineffective means of recruiting volunteers. Only about half of interviewees held interviews and took into account the skills that students brought to volunteer positions.

In chapters four and five, the authors and their interview subjects come down hardest on the practice of short-term service-learning projects and faculty who fail to communicate with service-learning partners. One of the most damning critiques of semester-long service projects comes from the voice of one nonprofit staffer: "once the semester is over . . . poof . . . they are gone. Sometimes the works are unfinished, sometimes they are not very good, and they left us a mess" (65). Another interviewee told a story of a professor who had made no effort to "seek an agency evaluation or to evaluate" the students' performance (92). These kinds of negative anecdotes pepper the book, reminding readers and practitioners that the structures of short-term service-learning projects often fail to generate effective partnerships.

Chapters six through eight begin the authors' move toward providing practices to address issues raised by community partners. In chapter six, Tryon, Hilgendorf, and Ian Scott, a Canadian community and urban planner, use a metaphor of romantic relationships to highlight the mutuality of institution-community relationships in service-learning partnerships. They cleverly compare some partnerships to "blind dates . . . set up by a department or a service learning office that might serve as both chaperone and matchmaker" (97). The authors assert, "mutual understanding is the touchstone of the relationship" (99). But Tryon, Hilgendorf, and Scott note that the chaperones and matchmakers are frequently missing in action. Students were often the primary and sometimes only connection to institutions (102). In chapter seven, authors Tryon, Stoecker, Charity Schmidt, and Cynthia Lin address the challenge of diversity in service-learning roles. The authors make valuable suggestions about the need for cultural competency and diversity training, but given the uniqueness of Madison's demographics, readers might view the chapter more for general principles.

Chapter eight, by Amy S. Mondloch, remains one of the most important features of the book. Mondloch, the executive director of the Grassroots Leadership College, a nonprofit community-organizing program in Madison, provides the only identified voice of a community partner in the book. Mondloch contends that community organizations "need to do a lot of thoughtful work before opening the door" to service learners (138). Mondloch encourages community organizations to consider how service learning fits within the organization's mission and vision (142). The difficulty with Mondloch's commentary is that her organization is geared towards education, which lines up much more cleanly with higher education's focus on learning. Still, even Mondloch claims that she "[thinks] twice before taking on any class projects. When we do decide to support a class project, it's because we've already begun to get to know the faculty member and trust that person" (144). The chapter begins and ends with a series of questions that nonprofits should ask themselves before engaging in a service-learning project: academics would be wise to consult this chapter and share its findings with partners before engaging in a service-learning relationship.

Chapters nine and ten conclude with recommendations: a set of principles and standards developed in collaboration with community organizations that participated in the interviews. While Stoecker, Dadit Hidayat, and Samuel Prastch's principles of commitment, communication, and compatibility should not surprise anyone who is familiar with service-learning literature, the book's qualitative methods ground these principles in the voices of community organizations. The authors make a strong case for the weakness of short-term service-learning projects, arguing that "commitment may be the most fundamental of the three Cs, for without a commitment to the community, there will be neither the energy to maintain good communication nor the will to develop training and screening mechanisms to assure compatibility" (149).

One major issue with the researchers' data is its generalizability. As one of their subjects noted in chapter three, Madison is "blessed with an abundance of volunteers" (44). Stoecker and Tryon admit this limitation in the last chapter of their book, with a call to readers to begin a similar conversation with local community organizations and avoid turning their results into "a boilerplate substitute for the process of hearing the voices of those in other communities" (186). The results, then, are likely to be less generalizable than other communities with lower volunteer involvement. The authors' findings do, however, suggest that if community partners express such levels of dissatisfaction with service-learning projects in a community known for activism and community involvement, other communities ought not be surprised when community organizations are reluctant to engage in service-learning relationships.

While admittedly limited by its focus on the Madison region, the book succeeds in giving voice to the frustrations, hopes, and desires of community partners engaged in service-learning partnerships and could serve as a framework for a range of regional research projects. Even if readers and service-learning practitioners don't replicate similar research, The Unheard Voices could serve as a valuable tool in helping establish initial relationships among community and academic partners. The book contains several useful heuristics for helping partners assess their capacity for service-learning partnerships. Chapters on why community partners engage in service learning and the chapter from a community partner's perspective could be valuable for graduate seminars on community literacy. Ultimately, The Unheard Voices suggests that institutions that fail to adequately commit to developing long-term relationships with community partners and fail to assess service-learning relationships may be harming more than helping community members.

Circulating Communities: The Tactics and Strategies of Community Publishing
Paula Mathieu, Steve Parks, and Tiffany Rousculp, eds.
Lanham: Lexington Books, 2011. 230 pp.

Reviewed by Beth Savoy
Kennesaw State University

From the start, editors Paula Mathieu, Steve Parks, and Tiffany Rousculp acknowledge the difficulties in defining and representing all types of what they call "community publishing" and "community writers." As they argue, rhetoric and composition has been a bit of a latecomer in noting the value of community publishing, as the field has much longer valued writing done for the purpose of attaining a college degree. Starting in the 1990s, though, scholarship began to consider "composition's extracurriculum" (Gere) by looking at writing beyond the classroom, especially writing that calls for public change and how that writing circulates (Wells), sometimes written by academics who have chosen to "go public" (Mortensen) as "public intellectuals" (Cushman) or by students engaging in service learning (Herzberg). While Mathieu, Parks, and Rousculp acknowledge the importance of these steps,   they ask for a shift in how we imagine our roles as writing teachers, particularly as we move from writing framed to be "about, with, and for" the community to community publishing being seen as "writing by the community."

More than that, Mathieu, Parks, and Rousculp believe that higher educational community partnerships can continue to exist so long as there is a shift in how these partnerships are maintained, especially as they believe that there needs to be consistent dialogue between both parties and a transparent effort in representing community writers as "marginal writers" and not simply "native informants." Therefore, *Circulating Communities: The Tactics and Strategies of Community Publishing* represents community writing as a type of participatory media that works to challenge dominant frameworks used by mainstream media to articulate the needs of poor or under-resourced populations. The text argues that "community writers" do this by challenging and/

or offering alternative outlets for expression in order to express their knowledge and worth to a larger audience, and in turn, encourage broader participation. The goal of the book is to represent scholarship about this type of "community writer" by investigating community publications created fully outside of the academy, exploring projects that work to inform composition and rhetoric classrooms by drawing from community-based publication projects, and asking us to consider how community publishing can take on an advocacy role as we link them to college students.

To summarize, the book is divided into three major sections. The first section includes four chapters that explore community publications that begin outside of the academy. Nick Pollard and Pat Smart are authors of the first chapter titled "Making Writing Accessible to All: The Federation of Worker Writers and Community Publishers and TheFED." Pollard and Smart discuss the coming together of the Federation of Worker Writers and Community Publishers (FWWCP) and TheFED from a writers' workshop at the Centerprise bookshop in 1976 London. The chapter itself explores the history and diverse publications of the group and argues that throughout its history, the group's central effort is the same—to make workers' voices heard and on their own terms. Paula Mathieu's chapter, "The Challenges of Circulation: International Networking of Homeless Publications," focuses on the challenges that community publications face as they work to circulate ideas within and beyond their communities, particularly the diverse circulation situations among street paper publications. Mathieu posits that these types of publications have the potential to do important advocacy work through helping impoverished and homeless people to establish networks, but that there are important steps that still need to be taken first. In "Respect, Writing, Community: Write Around Portland," Sara Guest with Hanna Neuschwander and Robyn Steely discusses the ways that Write Around Portland "serves 'underserved'" populations in the Portland area by offering participants a voice in their eight-to-ten week workshops since 1999. The chapter gives an overview of the program, history, and publications, discussing in much depth the publication process for their Write Around anthologies. The last chapter in this section, "Listen to My Story: The Transformative Possibilities of Storytelling in Immigrant Communities" by Mark Lyons, talks about Open Borders Project/Proyecto Sin Fronteras in North Philadelphia. In particular, Lyons discusses how their digital story program has woven together storytelling, writing, and technology to create audio stories that provide immigrants with computer and language skills while also creating a community around their classes. He also discusses the lessons they have learned from their digital storytelling program and how they are using their stories to organize public debate over immigration issues in the United States. These four chapters work to show how various community projects challenge dominant, mainstream media to give voices to various underrepresented populations.

The second section of the collection includes three chapters that draw from the work of community-based publication projects to inform rhetoric and composition classrooms. In "Oral Histories as Community Outreach: Toward a Deeper Understanding of a Rural Public Sphere," Laura Cella talks about her work at

Shippensburg University in Pennsylvania, particularly an oral history project written by first-year writing students for a community member of their choice. She discusses the goals that were met and unmet by publishing the oral history projects in a journal and what she and her students learned by working on the project. Rachel Meads in "Unfinished: A Story of *sine cera*, a Community Publications in Process" discusses the Salt Lake Community College (SLCC) Community Writing Center's annual anthology of their DiverseCity Writing Series (DWS) called *sine cera*. In particular, she gives the history and purpose of the program and its anthologies, the changes and challenges it has faced, and its current challenges, including how they can continue to imagine how higher educational community partnerships can continue to be mutually beneficial. North Carolina's Durham County Library is the location where Abels, Clemons, Wilson, Winters, and Woods describe the six-year history and evolution of a program that pairs teens with volunteer writing coaches from UNC-Chapel Hill and Duke writing centers to publish their work. Like other chapters, "Here in this Place: Write On! Of Durham, North Carolina" describes the rewarding work volunteers have found in helping enable marginalized students find their voice.

Finally, the third section of the collection includes four chapters that investigate how community publishing can take on an advocacy role as it is linked to college students. In "Sharing Space: Collaborative Programming Within and Between Communities," Case, Knepler, and Soni from the Neighborhood Writing Alliance (NWA) in Chicago explore the history of their collaborations and partnerships. Case, Knepler, and Soni discuss the trials and errors they experienced with collaborating but place much emphasis on the overall importance and value of such collaborations. Richard Louth in "Katrina in Their Own Words: Collecting, Creating, and Publishing Writing on the Storm" writes about the radio program "Katrina: In Their Own Words," as it enabled students impacted by Hurricane Katrina to broadcast their stories on the Southeastern Louisiana University's radio station, KSLU. He considers the challenges and rewards of writing and teaching writing about the storm—for himself and his students. "Writers Speaking Out: The Challenges of Community Publishing from Spaces of Confinement" by Tobi Jacobi and Elliot Johnston reflects on the SpeakOut! Writing workshops for youth and adult writers confined to correctional and rehabilitation centers in Fort Collins, Colorado, and sponsored by the Community Literacy Center at Colorado State University. The chapter discusses the process of publication of the SpeakOut! journal as well as the unique challenges of circulation and reception the journal faces. Finally, the last chapter, "A Bunch of Us Beg to Differ!: Queer Community Literacy and Rhetorics to Civic Pride" by A.V. Luce, discusses how university, art, and community activists in Syracuse responded to anti-gay hate speech in 2009 with an online collaborative photo project published on Blogspot. Luce posits that understanding the "community" part of the "community publishing" process may be just as important as the product it captures. These four chapters in particular work to show that collaboration among many is key in realizing the advocacy role of community publishing.

On the one hand, the book's biggest strength might be in its work to represent multiple types of community publishing projects working in mutually benefitting partnerships with various underrepresented community writers. This diversity, as well as the decision to break the book into three different sections with three different goals, opens its potential usefulness to multiple readers inside and outside of the classroom, field of rhetoric and composition, university, and United States, as the book shows that these projects are often sponsored by collaborations between multiple people and organizations, including universities and communities. Additionally, these multiple readers could potentially gain various types of wisdom from the book: the histories and publication processes of many of these types of organizations lends pragmatic wisdom to readers, discussions of both achievements and shortcomings offer a sense of community that comes with such honesty, and the book is a step in connecting the various community publishing projects in the book to each other and other audiences. On the other hand, for a book that focuses on community publishing as a form of participatory media, it would be nice to see more examples of digital participatory media. While a couple of pieces focus on the use of technology to publish audio histories and stories, only Luce's piece really focuses on the power of the internet to connect us in the 21st century. The editors explain in the introduction their decision to focus most on the power of print media, particularly regarding the populations it reaches and the reverence it carries, but I wonder if a look at digital participatory media might aid in helping publishing reach a new level of that advocacy role the editors mention.

Zines in Third Space: Radical Cooperation and Borderlands Rhetoric
Adela C. Licona
Albany: SUNY P, 2012. 207 pp.

Reviewed by Jenna Vinson
University of Massachusetts Lowell

In her 2011 review of rhetorician Adela C. Licona's documentary work, Marianna Grohowski hoped readers of the *Community Literacy Journal* would be inspired by Licona's efforts to make visible non-academic community literacies while also performing multimodal, community-relevant composition. Readers of the *CLJ* will be happy to learn that Licona's latest publication continues to emphasize the value and impact of community literacies. Her book, *Zines in Third Space: Radical Cooperation and Borderlands Rhetoric*, provides activists, researchers, and educators with 1) a new theoretical framework through which to analyze community literacies and coalitional practices and 2) a vibrant genre to consider for community literacy projects and rhetorical analysis: zines.

Zines are self-published and often locally-circulated booklets that are made up of words and images. The term "zine" derives from magazines and fanzines. However, as Licona explains, zines are a distinct genre characterized by content that challenges societal norms and dominant ways of thinking. In addition, the authors of zines—or zinesters—refuse "to wait for permission or acceptance" to write, publish, or circulate these texts (20). In conducting research for this book, Licona analyzed zines from the 1980s and 1990s that were donated to the Sallie Bingham Center Special Collections Library at Duke University. In her book, Licona argues for the value of third-space zines as sites for rhetorical study, coalitional community building, and the "hopeful potential" of social change. "Third space" is a tricky concept that Licona describes as "the abyss beyond dualisms" (8). Licona explains that third space can reference a physical location (e.g., a place in-between two other places such as a borderland), a methodology (i.e., a way of reading a text to look for ambiguities or challenges to established dichotomies), and a practice (i.e., being conscious of both/and possibilities as opposed to either/or distinctions). Licona asserts that the tactics, or borderlands rhetorics, of third-space zinesters move us past marginalizing and reductive binaries to both/and consciousness and productive ambiguities. Zines potentially resist dominant dichotomies, build coalition, share lived knowledge, and promote grassroots literacies.

The book includes five chapters. In the first chapter, "Borderlands Rhetorics and Third-Space Sites," Licona introduces readers to zines and carefully delimits the scope of her study. She explains that she searched the Duke University collection for zines that were collaboratively authored by what she calls third-space subjects—authors who are feminist, queer, and/or of-color and who use the genre to articulate shared goals for egalitarian social change. By focusing on third-space print zines, Licona writes that she can analyze the spatialized literacy practices of people collectively working toward social justice in the specific areas where the zines circulate. Then, Licona sets up the theoretical framework of her study, drawing from the critical terms and insights of Chicana scholars Gloria Anzaldúa, Chela Sandoval, Emma Pérez as well as feminist cultural geographer Doreen Massey. Scholars who similarly seek to assess the contributions and strategies of marginalized rhetorics will appreciate Licona's distinctions between criticism and coalitional consciousness, dichotomies and third space, and homogeneity and community.

In the second chapter, "The Role of Imagination in Challenging Everyday Dominations," Licona builds on Chandra Mohanty and Gloria Anzaldúa's emphasis on the importance of imagination as a coalition-building tool. She examines how zinesters imagine new ways they (and others in their communities) can connect via lived experience, shared knowledges, and collective resistance to social injustice. Licona illustrates different strategies zinesters use to invite and inspire coalitional activism including visual/discursive interventions in issues that readers across lines of difference would find upsetting (e.g., Nike's exploitation of Vietnamese laborers). Licona describes how zinesters' explicit calls for multi-racial collaboration on an issue or action and code switching practices allow multiply literate readers to engage. Readers of *CLJ* will especially enjoy the section "Community Scribes: Lived and Relational Knowledges and Community Literacies" as Licona powerfully and persuasively demonstrates how zines challenge the tyranny of "expert" or "authorized" knowledges by, instead, sharing and valuing lived knowledges—or the personal stories and perspectives shared by people who experience the things they are writing about.

In chapter three "Embodied Intersections" Licona continues to illustrate how zinesters value and circulate "embodied knowledge," or ways of knowing based on lived experience, in order to build community literacy of socio-political issues that need to be addressed. In this chapter, she draws on feminist theories of emotion, subjectivity, and body politics to explore the role of emotion (which she represents as "e-motion") in zines. Licona demonstrates how zinesters "integrate emotion into their knowledge claims," particularly love and anger (65). This is my favorite part of the book as Licona shows us example after example of feminist zinesters using personal narratives, hyperbolic claims, and visual representations to call out cultural icons and practices that piss. them. off. Licona persuades readers that explicit anger is a valuable third-space rhetorical tactic in that e-motion invites coalition (among others who know/feel/live likewise), informs meaning making, and motivates action. Also important to this chapter is Licona's theorization of a tactic of social critique called "reverso." Reverso includes the discursive and visual strategies zinesters use to reverse the often oppressive and divisive gaze on minoritized people to, instead, highlight and render abnormal those ways of looking and their accordant practices. This often involves questioning "expert" discourses—such as medical officials' concerns about "fat" and the psychological treatments for addiction—as well as the explicit refusal to be silent about sexual abuse.

In chapter four, "Queer-y-ing Consumption and Production," Licona turns her attention to how zines resist dominant norms for consumption and production in our postmodern, globalized society through the "creative and critical inquiry and class-consciousness" that she terms "queer-y-ing" (100). Queer-y-ing, as performed in zines, may include destabilizing dominant understandings of gender and sexuality, promoting ambiguity, re-appropriating familiar images (like Barbie) to question social norms, making visible inequitable and exploitative production practices (such as the production of beef), and re-telling history to reclaim bi (or seemingly bi) female historical figures. Licona also demonstrates that the genre of the zine itself challenges "first-order" consumption practices wherein the consumer purchases a product or intellectual property from the producer/retailer. For example, zinesters often reproduce content from other writers/media without permission in the aim of broad readership and accessible education. In this way, zines challenge mass production and consumption materially and discursively.

Chapter 5 is Licona's epilogue, entitled "Third-Space Theory and Borderlands Rhetorics." In this chapter, Licona reiterates the importance of third space and borderlands rhetoric and explains why she studied zines as her primary example of these rhetorical practices. She offers us insight into who she imagines will take up these ideas about third space—rhetoricians, cultural theorists, feminist scholars, and anyone who needs to "identify and explain creative resistances and responses to marginalizing structures and practices" (136). While Licona does not offer us any additional examples from zines in this chapter, she does offer rich examples of third space subjectivity and borderlands rhetoric by situating herself as a third-space subject. She shares childhood memories from living in the U.S./Mexico border region, personal/academic reactions to Gloria Anzaldúa's work, and her admiration and love for the third-space experiences of her father who taught her so much. In short, Licona models embodied rhetoric that refuses a dichotomy between the personal and the academic.

One of the primary reasons this book is so valuable is because it demonstrates how community literacy is promoted, engaged, and circulated in the multimodal genre of zines. I can imagine literacy researchers collecting and studying zines from their communities as a way of knowing more about the literacy practices therein. In addition, Licona's careful attention to the visual and discursive representations in zines will appeal to those interested in visual rhetoric. In fact, the excerpts I used from Licona's book in my undergraduate Visual Rhetoric course this past semester sparked exciting discussions of how visual representations can perform social criticism[1]. In a brief footnote to her epilogue, Licona explains that she has used zines in the classroom as a way to encourage students to bring their everyday knowledges and lived histories into their academic inquiry and writing. Assignments that call for students to collaboratively construct zines with their classmates or people in the non-academic community could encourage community-relevant undergraduate research and writing projects. Although the theoretical framing of the book might be difficult for undergraduates, individual chapters—such as chapters 2 and 3—may pair nicely with a unit on zines and other non-academic, community-based genres. This could prompt students to think about the civic importance of writing for social justice.

There is also much to admire and learn from the way in which Licona organizes and writes her book. From the opening dedication to the "acknowledgement of gifts of knowledge" to the body chapters that follow, Zines in Third Space models academic scholarship that recognizes and values community as a site for the sharing and learning of new knowledge and literacy practices. Furthermore, Licona uses language to interrupt readers' understanding of certain terms. Licona writes, "In my work, I play with language. I always have. It is serious play though which I am able to reimagine language's potential" (6). Using strategic punctuation and diction, Licona encourages us to re(en)vision the meaning and impact of specific words. As one example, she writes, "Like many third-space subjects, I have needed to read and interpret con/texts, and reread and reinterpret con/texts, in multiple directions" (7). Here, Licona interrupts any simple understanding of context—the circumstance of/around something—to prompt readers to consider the drawbacks of the texts she was assigned in elementary school. She describes creatively reading between the lines of Dick and Jane books for places of recognition as a bilingual, Chicana first grader. Licona's practice of word play is a performance of the very borderlands rhetorics she identifies and analyzes in zines.

It feels important to end this review by situating myself in third space. I am—at one and the same time—Licona's reviewer, Licona's mentee, Licona's former colleague, and Licona's friend. I have worked with her in the non-academic community to build relationships between youth organizations and academic researchers and I have worked with her in the ivory tower on my dissertation, her scholarship, and campus events. Writing this review has been just one more opportunity to blur the imagined boundaries between each of those roles while learning and being challenged by Licona's ways of thinking.

Endnotes

1. Those who are interested in reading an excellent example of a zine should consult issue 8.1 of the *Community Literacy Journal,* which includes a zine collaboratively produced by youth activists from Chicago, Detroit, San Francisco, and Tucson.

The Word and the World: The Cultural Politics of Literacy in Brazil
Lesley Bartlett
New Jersey: Hampton P, 2010. 232 pp.

Reviewed by Katie Silvester and Anne-Marie Hall
University of Arizona

Lesley Bartlett's *The Word and the World* offers *CLJ* readers a global, comparative perspective on Freirean-inspired community literacy work. Based on 27-months of ethnographic data collected in Brazilian literacy programs, Bartlett's book constructively rethinks Freire's critical literacy pedagogy in its native context as well as the so-called "consequences" of literacy in the larger context of development discourses engineered by international non-governmental organizations. Drawing on a feminist poststructural critique of power and socio-cultural theories of literacy, the book develops three major lines of argument: 1) literacy by itself does not create change; therefore, 2) any discussion of the impact of literacy must include consideration of the social contexts of literate practices and policies, and 3) the study of critical pedagogy as a situated practice reveals the limitations of Freirean praxis especially around issues of knowledge, power, and the limits of dialogue. Chapters 3, 4, and 5 reflect what Bartlett describes as the "ethnographic heart" of the book, a deeply qualitative analysis of literacy ideologies and praxis among teachers and students in one Brazilian community literacy program. From this analysis, Bartlett concludes that while Freirean critical literacy pedagogy has done much to expand a socio-cultural critique of literacy in people's lives, the insistence among practitioners that critical literacy work will lead to people's empowerment is teleological rather than actually transformative, and hence problematic. Ultimately, Bartlett argues for "new critical literacy studies," as future work that will refresh Freirean critical literacy praxis by disrupting older, limiting notions of what local literacy is and does by carefully critiquing language inequality through power relations both in the classroom and beyond. Consequently *The Word and the World* has relevance for *CLJ* readers looking for a more global perspective, as Bartlett demonstrates how community literacy praxis does, can, and should evolve internationally. At the same time, this book is of particular relevance to literacy workers in the field given its discussion of the obstacles that local educators face when they try to enact Freirean pedagogy.

As two reviewers with experience conducting ethnographic literacy research in international contexts, we engage in dialogue around *The Word and the World* below. By engaging in this dialogue we hope to address what is surprising and relevant about this work for other literacy researchers and scholars. The review considers three questions in light of our reading: What is Bartlett's criticism of Freire? What is the most surprising aspect of her argument? How does this research inform community literacy?

What is Lesley Bartlett's criticism of Freire?

AMH: Bartlett merely reads Freire "against the grain" through the lens of feminist poststructural theory and sociocultural theories of literacy. She is ever respectful of Freire's enormous contributions to pedagogy and critical literacy and considers Freire almost a "saint." Still she examines his pedagogy (which she argues is really more a philosophy or social theory than a teaching method) as an *ideology*, a system of ideas and beliefs, and then she proceeds to study the struggles that occur when his pedagogy is implemented by literacy educators in Brazil who are ostensibly trained in Freirean theories. I suspect that one thing Bartlett discovered in Brazil is also true of many educators in the US who use Paulo Freire—they are mostly familiar with his early work, *The Pedagogy of the Oppressed,* and his ideas about problem-posing education and the banking concept of education. Most know little of his middle work (the talking books) or his later work such as *Pedagogy of Hope*, in which Freire reflects on the twenty years since *Pedagogy of the Oppressed* was published. In this later work, he cautions that he never intended Freirean pedagogy to become a methodology, and he argues that it is not just learning content that matters but also the understanding of the *whys* of the positions or places in which we find ourselves. Finally, it is the added elaboration on the necessity of hope in our lives that really bookends this work with his earlier, better known book.

Additionally, Bartlett argues that Freire's concept of power leads him to "construct unproductive dichotomies" such as dominant knowledge/popular knowledge, teachers as authoritarian/emancipatory, and education as oppressive/liberatory (117). Bartlett demonstrates in Chapter 5 that these dichotomies stymied the work of the teachers in her study. She uses Foucault to broaden Freire's discussion of power, citing Foucault's argument that power is continually exercised by all people but for different ends and outcomes. Thus it circulates constantly. By deconstructing such binary approaches for the classroom, Bartlett argues that Freire's philosophical pedagogy overgeneralizes power as possession and universalizes oppression.

I was particularly impressed with Bartlett's nuanced discussion of dialogue. While aware that poststructuralists critique dialogue as the "hegemony of reasonableness," Bartlett troubles the notion that teacher-student dialogue does much more than move a student toward a "correct" readings of a text or situation. Dialogue in a literacy education project is never innocent and frequently, well-intentioned teachers ignore the politics of linguistic interaction, thinking somehow that correct thinking and knowledge lead to emancipation (142).

KS: Bartlett's exploration of Freirean critical literacy pedagogy as ideology is interesting, especially in the way she asks us to think carefully about what we, as literacy educators and researchers, mean by our educational projects. Early on in the book, Bartlett expands the scope of educational projects as not just skill-driven initiatives, but also socio-cultural and political initiatives. Accordingly, Bartlett defines literacy programs as "durable (but not permanent) constellations of *institutions, financial resources, social actors, ideologies, discourses, pedagogies, and theories of knowledge and learning*" that shape the way people think about schooling and its purpose (52). Her overall argument is undergirded by an ideological view of literacy, which Bartlett borrows from seminal works in New Literacy Studies. In these works, two competing views of literacy are often scrutinized for their social implications. The first view is of literacy as "autonomous." That means reading and writing work independently from other social factors, in people's overall development. An "ideological" view of literacy, on the other hand, argues for a more situated perspective of people's development wherein the cultural understanding and practice of literacy plays a constitutive role. For Bartlett, as well as other New Literacy Studies scholars, it's not literacy's outcomes that are as significant or as interesting as people's *beliefs* about what literacy is and what literacy does. Bartlett's research centers on these ideologically framed questions—what people believe about literacy and how they enact these beliefs in everyday practice—in the context of critical literacy projects in the birthplace of Freirean pedagogy, Brazil.

Students' and teachers' ideological views of literacy are in conflict in Bartlett's book. The "ethnographic heart" of her research is grounded in observation and interview data and qualitative analysis of teachers' views of critical literacy as a powerful, social transformer. Yet, similar research of student views reveals some disturbance of this ideal in actual practice. For example, while teachers lauded Freirean pedagogy for its emancipatory potential and its power to "alphabetize in order to politicize", students' views of reading and writing index literacy knowledge as "good manners" and "speaking well," not mobilization for social change. Additionally, Bartlett found that at the level of classroom practice, Freirean ideals fall short and that the actual dynamics of power, knowledge, and speech in the classroom do not always reflect teachers' perceived goal of critical literacy to emancipate students' from social inequality. Rather, classroom activity often reified the status quo as students and teachers seemed to lack the skills to manage Freirean dialogue effectively. In Bartlett's observations teachers often let students' unexamined experiences drive classroom discussions in circles out of fear that intervening in students' understanding of their own experiences would be a forceful imposition of "schooled" knowledge onto "popular" knowledge. The middle chapters of the book are mostly preoccupied with the problems of managing transformative, Freirean dialogue and negotiating experience and knowledge in the literacy classroom. These chapters help to support Bartlett and others' ideological view of literacy and the idea that literacy teaching and learning is more than just the transference of reading and writing skills. Bartlett's work reminds me of the deeply ideological implications of the work we do as literacy educators, especially when our motives seem to spring from good intentions and even claim to be transformative.

What is Bartlett's most surprising argument?

KS: For me, Bartlett's most surprising arguments come in Chapter 4, "Education and Shame," where she highlights the overlooked dimension of emotions, especially shame, in enabling the cultural production of language inequality. First, Bartlett's use of Bourdieu's theoretical apparatus of field, capital, and habitus in this chapter is worth mentioning for the particular light these terms shed on language inequality in general. Through Bourdieu, Bartlett argues that people encounter literacy in linguistic fields, or spaces of linguistic practice, where different forms of oral and literate production are legitimated differently. These forms are composed of various language resources, which have symbolic exchange value that, much like monetary currency, differs across various social fields. Bartlett calls the symbolic exchange value of people's language resources, linguistic capital. She draws on Bourdieu's term, habitus, to talk about the limits of people's linguistic capital. Habitus in this sense, points to people's socialization into subjectivities, or habits of mind and body and language solidified in years of layered social experience. A person's habitus limits her or his mobilization of linguistic resources as capital since the language usage of differently socialized subjectivities is considered more or less acceptable to differently privileged listeners in and across historical spaces of language use. Therefore, Bartlett suggests that the concepts of field, capital, and habitus provide essential theoretical terminology for thinking about the value of literacy tied to the social contexts in which it is situated. For Bourdieu there can be no universally significant form of linguistic capital, for all language is situated. However, Bartlett departs from Bourdieu on this point, arguing that while theoretically language and literacy are situated practices, many people continue to believe in and desire a language and literacy concept that is more universal. In her work, the desire for a universal and autonomous literacy is tied to language shame, that is shame over vernacular ways of talking and being in the world, and is repeatedly expressed by the informants in her study as strong motivator for taking up literacy work in the community.

I think it's important for literacy workers and researchers to think carefully about how literacy practice is socially, discursively, symbolically, and even emotionally mediated in the classroom and beyond and how this mediated language practice reflects not only local attitudes and beliefs about language and people, but also global attitudes and beliefs about language and people embedded in the local. Bartlett structures the narrative of her research by, at first, taking a careful and critical look at a particular pedagogy and then measuring that pedagogy against the language beliefs, practices, and emotional experiences of actual people in local contexts where people's international development, their development relative to other people's development globally, is a national priority. We need more research, like Bartlett's, in the field of community literacy to make the connections—among cultural language attitudes and people's emotional encounters with language, and among community practices and global language policies—more apparent.

AMH: I was particularly struck by Bartlett's critique of the ubiquitous "literacy myth"— that "narrative of the redeeming effects of literacy" that Bartlett's fieldwork shows is highly overrated. The students in these literacy projects in Brazil were not led to conscientization or to social change by this Freirean/critical pedagogy. Rather what truly benefited students was the experience of being in a setting where social networks and relationships cultivated in school truly improved their economic standing—not the "content" learned in school. I think the romanticism of critical pedagogy is thoroughly disrupted in this text. Literacy contributes to the expansion of social networks and it was those relationships that had an effect on economic mobility. In community literacy programs in the US, I think of how demonstrating a strong work ethic, meeting other people, and improving self-esteem all contribute to empowerment. We need to be more conscious of the affordances literacies offer people and also the capricious ways they are used and linked. I guess I would say this is a point worth repeating: many critical pedagogues who consider themselves Freiristas continue to believe that literacy will conscientize individuals and lead to social change. Or worse, political activism. But for those who work in community literacy programs, it is wise to realize that this is an overly simplified and naïve understanding of critical pedagogy. Bartlett's rupturing of this particular literacy myth is powerful. Literacy is ecological and supports the elaborate relationships between people and their environments. Literacy practices, then, are directly tied to their local contexts where surviving on a daily basis is far more important than engaging in intellectually-challenging literacy pursuits. And I do not mean to romanticize poverty in any way by suggesting that the literacy skills needed to survive involve complex mental strategies and are, indeed, enough. However, it bears saying that there are ways of knowing that are highly skilled and that don't involve "official" constructions of literacy.

In what ways can community literacy be informed by Bartlett's work?

KS: Readers of *CLJ* might wonder about congruence between Bartlett's critique of critical pedagogy and community literacy. They might ask, in what ways can/should community literacy (or a working definition of community literacy, at least) inform or be informed by Bartlett's work? I think that we could argue that Bartlett's critique of Bourdieu and her focus on the dimensions of emotion, especially shame, in the cultural production of power in education and language inequality may resonate with work in community literacy that seeks to build connections between marginalized speaker/ writers and a larger community. Additionally, Bartlett's critique of Freire around notions of experience, knowledge production, and dialogue are key issues being worked out in the more recent scholarship of community literacy specialists, especially in Linda Flower's work regarding the rhetoric of public engagement and Elenore Long's work on the rhetoric of local publics. Certainly, both critical pedagogy and community literacy scholars have something to gain in critically and reflexively considering how teaching, tutoring, or mentoring practices, literacy sponsorship, and teleology in the field reify universal and/or autonomous notions of literacy. Furthermore, a better understanding of our own and others' emotional attachment to different ideas about literacy is needed in order to more fully explore how universal literacies operate locally. But aside from theory, literacy teaching and learning continues to engage people politically, culturally, and economically for better or for worse.

AMH: Community literacy workers need to continue to see literacy education as a political struggle and always work to create more egalitarian relations in the classroom between students and teachers. It is reasonable to assume that literacy has the potential to make things less unequal; however, it is also important for educators to realize that school-based notions of literacy do not automatically translate into empowerment for learners. Bartlett does an excellent job in critiquing notions of improved self-esteem as somehow resulting in "empowerment." In fact, it was not literacy per se that improved students' lives. Her data showed that literacy had no predictable effect on students because the students applied literacy to such divergent ends. Nor did most students become increasingly economically mobile; indeed, the link between literacy schooling and improved employment was weak. Finally, rethinking power as something that circulates and is "simultaneously exercised and experienced by all" (170) is particularly grounding for community literacy workers. I agree with Bartlett that we need to question the Freirean belief that conscientization, or a full critical knowledge unfiltered by reigning discursive structures and regimes of truth, is possible (174).

PARLOR PRESS
EQUIPMENT FOR LIVING

Congratulations to These Award Winners!

GenAdmin: Theorizing WPA Identities in the Twenty-First Century
Colin Charlton, Jonikka Charlton, Tarez Samra Graban, Kathleen J. Ryan, & Amy Ferdinandt Stolley
Winner of the Best Book Award, Council of Writing Program Adminstrators (July, 2014)

Mics, Cameras, Symbolic Action: Audio-Visual Rhetoric for Writing Teachers
Bump Halbritter
Winner of the Distinguished Book Award from Computers and Composition (May, 2014)

New Releases

First-Year Composition: From Theory to Practice
Edited by Deborah Coxwell-Teague & Ronald F. Lunsford. 420 pages.
Twelve of the leading theorists in composition studies answer, in their own voices, the key question about what they hope to accomplish in a first-year composition course. Each chapter, and the accompanying syllabi, provides rich insights into the classroom practices of these theorists.

A Rhetoric for Writing Program Administrators
Edited by Rita Malenczyk. 471 pages.
Thirty-two contributors delineate the major issues and questions in the field of writing program administration and provide readers new to the field with theoretical lenses through which to view major issues and questions.

www.parlorpress.com

DEPAUL UNIVERSITY

DEPARTMENT OF
WRITING, RHETORIC, & DISCOURSE

Master of Arts Degrees in
NEW MEDIA STUDIES
WRITING, RHETORIC, & DISCOURSE
with concentrations in
Professional & Technical Writing
Teaching Writing & Language

Graduate certificate in TESOL
Combined BA/MA in WRD

Bachelor of Arts in **WRITING, RHETORIC, & DISCOURSE**
Minor in **Professional Writing**

 facebook.com/DePaulWRD   @DePaulWRD

WRD.DEPAUL.EDU

www.ingramcontent.com/pod-product-compliance
Lightning Source LLC
Chambersburg PA
CBHW031601170426
43196CB00032B/982